*Social Development in Times
of Economic Uncertainty*

Social Development in Times of Economic Uncertainty

PROCEEDINGS OF THE XXTH INTERNATIONAL
CONFERENCE ON SOCIAL WELFARE
HONG KONG
July 18–22, 1980

Published 1981
for the INTERNATIONAL COUNCIL ON SOCIAL WELFARE
by COLUMBIA UNIVERSITY PRESS
NEW YORK

Library of Congress Cataloging in Publication Data

International Conference on Social Welfare (20th
 : 1980 : Hong Kong)
  Social development in times of economic uncertainty.

  Includes bibliographical references.
  1. Quality of life—Congresses. 2. Social policy—Congresses. 3. Social service—Congresses. I. International Council on Social Welfare. II. Title.
HN25.I57   1980   361.6′1   81-3884
ISBN 0-231-05326-6   AACR2

Columbia University Press
New York   Guildford, Surrey

Copyright © 1981 Columbia University Press
All rights reserved
Printed in the United States of America

Printed on permanent and durable acid-free paper.

Contents

The Opening of the XXth International Conference on
  Social Welfare   vii
  Introduction   *Lucien Mehl*   vii
  Remarks   *Y. F. Hui*   x
  Address   *His Excellency Sir Jack Cater*, K.B.E., J.P.   xii
  Vote of Thanks   *Ingrid Gelinek*   xvii

Conference Working Document   *James R. Dumpson*   1
Hard Times and the Search for a Frugal Utopia   *John F. Jones*   34
Recent World Development and Its Impact on the Poor in the
  Third World   *Andre Franco Montoro*   52
People Are the Policy   *William A. Dyson*   64
Social Welfare Development in Hong Kong in the 1970s
  Harold Ho   103
Refugees in Southeast Asia   *Hari Brissimi*   111
Intercountry Adoption   *Hansa Apparao and Najma M.
  Goriawalla*   126
Development of Collaboration among Various Service Sectors
  at the Delivery Level
  Part I.   *H. Philip Hepworth*   150
  Part II.   *Moacyr Velloso Caraoso de Oliveira*   161
The René Sand Award
  Getting Back to People: a Bid for a New Approach   *Gradus
  Hendriks*   167
Summary and Review of the XXth International Conference
  on Social Welfare   *James R. Dumpson*   182

Appendix
  Countries Represented   199
  International Council on Social Welfare Executive
    Committee   200
  Program Committee   201
  International Staff   201
  Hong Kong Organizing Committee   201

The Opening of the XXth International Conference on Social Welfare

INTRODUCTION

LUCIEN MEHL
PRESIDENT, INTERNATIONAL COUNCIL ON SOCIAL WELFARE

TRADITION EXPECTS the President of the ICSW to present his opinion on the subject of the theme of this the XXth Conference: "Social Development in Times of Economic Uncertainty."

In agreement with the organizers of this conference and without breaking from tradition, I felt that it would be better to restrict myself to brief considerations, since you have on the one hand the remarkable document by James R. Dumpson, for which we must congratulate him warmly, and on the other hand you will be hearing the interesting comments of John F. Jones, Senator Andre Franco Montoro, and William A. Dyson to whom I extend thanks on your behalf.

In order to avoid repetition I shall proceed like some pupils and not touch on this subject. One means of reaching this negative result is to ask oneself what is the meaning of economic certainty, since the theme of this conference relates to uncertainty.

Thus I ask this subversive question: can we trace periods of economic certainty in history?

These would be periods when short- or medium-term provisions would prove to be justified, where plans or programs for agriculture, urbanization, industrialization, and development in general would have been executed more effectively; that is to say, periods when policy-makers would control the economic system. They could also be periods of *laissez faire*, of liberal economy where the contractors would show a justifiable confidence in the future and would see their anticipations justified, times without crisis cycles, without depression, without Black Fridays, without moroseness.

Even if I were able to draw up an inventory of such periods, I would spare you that. If one is inclined to be indulgent to soothsayers, experts, businessmen, and politicians one is able to come across a certain number of these periods. In any case, they are always relatively short. However, there is indeed such a period which is well known to all of us: the last quarter of this century, 1950–74, a time of relative certainty and appreciable prosperity but one really seen only in the industrialized countries.

The perverse pupil could make the observation, too, that certainty could also mean poverty or even starvation. During the Ice Age, the cave man knew that if he did not kill the bear he would die of hunger, and a similarly precarious situation has existed since time immemorial, and it seems that it will be prolonged. One could list many examples from history of this certainty of poverty, even, unfortunately, contemporary examples.

Our present economic uncertainty is only partial. We are sure, or almost sure, that the slow or nonexistent growth, unemployment, and inflation will continue for years, perhaps for more than a decade in the countries where the economy was in the past the most prosperous. Thus it would be imprudent to assimilate certainty and prosperity: uncertainty and periods of crisis. Moreover, pioneers and innovators are acting in a climate of uncertainty, and they are able to obtain fruitful results for themselves and others.

Aware of his incapacity in treating this subject, the pupil will put forward as his pretext the unsure meaning of uncertainty in order to gain time and hide his ignorance. "Uncertainty, what does it mean?" he asks. It is the opposite of certainty. The state of certainty in the case of a contemporary or forthcoming event means that one has complete information at one's disposal on the situation or event. This is true with an eclipse or a space voyage. Everything is based on Newton's system and is determined and foreseeable (at least in principle).

In economics, certainty implies that one has an adequate, realistic model at one's disposition and that with the help of this model one is able to make sufficiently precise provisions and feasible decisions which will ultimately lead to the researched result and aimed-for goal.

Let us imagine, however, that we do not have complete information at our disposal and that we have to call on probabilists' reasonings and formulas. Is this, then, the state of uncertainty? Not necessarily. One knows that a strong probability is about the same as a certainty and that economic models are more or less probabilistic.

Real uncertainty, profound uncertainty, appears when one is unable to assign probabilities to eventualities. Even this is not the worst of situations because if we are able to determine the list of eventualities even without coefficient probability, we can still define a strategy; that is to say, we can set in advance the approach to be adopted in each hypothesis. The uncertainty which is more grave exists when one is incapable of enumerating all the eventualities.

Finally, the worst situation is to ignore the fact that one is ignoring certain eventualities. That is, unless it is a situation where one does not want to be reminded of what one knows has already happened or does not want to know what will happen. The last hypothesis is appropriately applicable to the present economic situation, which has serious consequences for the future, especially for social development.

But these considerations do not satisfy the examiner. He asks the pupil to explain at least his last affirmation. The pupil replies that before he fulfills this task he wants to have social development defined. The examiner, terrified, for he does not feel capable of formulating such a definition, gives the pupil a zero. He reprimands and reminds the pupil that he was to have written his work on neither economic uncertainty nor social development but on the interrelationship between these two concepts. This is, of course, with what this conference will deal. I am convinced of the great importance of the matters which we are going to discuss during the coming days in relation to social development.

Economic uncertainty may have as an effect the increase of economic decline, and it is, moreover, a factor of reinforcement for inequality.

In order to enhance social development, social policy must perhaps come from new conceptions and put new instruments into operation. Frugal utopias—and almost all utopias from those of Sir Thomas More to those of Tommaso Campanella as well as the others—can they become realities or should one constitute a set of anti-utopian means? In the first hypothesis, that of a frugal utopia presented if not as an immediate object at least as an ideal to which one should reach, one hopes that people will awake to the consciousness of the situation and accept a certain moderation in their wishes and have a greater feeling of solidarity. In the second hypothesis, that I will call the anti-utopia, to which Keynes after Bernard de Mandeville resigned himself, it is necessary to make allowances for human weakness, selfishness, and ignorance. For this reason, one should count almost as much on vices as on virtues; one should not hope or request too much but have a strong position on what is asked.

Perhaps there is a dialectic solution that could overcome the antagonism between utopia and anti-utopia, I do not think I have found it. In all events, I am sure that the conference will help to throw light on the ways to be offered to social development.

REMARKS

Y. F. HUI

CHAIRMAN, ORGANIZING COMMITTEE OF THE XXTH INTERNATIONAL CONFERENCE ON SOCIAL WELFARE

OPENING THE XXth International Conference on Social Welfare in the presence of so many learned visitors from abroad is a very special and honored occasion for Hong Kong. It is indeed a unique experience for Hong Kong to host for the first time a global welfare conference, having the entire ICSW family with us. The occasion is given further significance in that it has taken exactly one decade since the 1970 Manila conference for the ICSW conference to be held once again in the Asian and Western Pacific region.

The 1970s, in which economic progress everywhere in the world has not always been matched by social stability, have created universal difficulties of social adaptation, of harmonizing "growth" with "social justice." In view of the fact that social development has been, and will be, taking place amid serious limitations posed by economic constraints, it is necessary to seek innovative social measures and approaches for tackling emerging social problems. It is against this backdrop that the theme of the ICSW conference acquires special meaning. We of the social welfare discipline have the obligation to assess whether the objectives and parameters of social welfare need to be altered in view of the economic uncertainty of the 1980s, and to identify strategies and methods by which we can influence the direction of those institutions and systems that have an impact on social development.

The explicit purpose of this conference is to offer an opportunity for all of us to reflect on issues of common concern, to examine the premise in which social development stands, and to identify directions in which social development and social welfare agencies should move. In a quest such as this, it is inevitable that certain ambiguities and generalities could come up. This is akin to the anxiety commonly entertained in respect to forums of this size and nature; that is, they are strong on generalities but weak on specifics. This is a challenge which I feel this august assembly should take up, so that at the end of our conference, we shall be able not only to make an accurate diagnosis, but also to offer a concrete prescription and prognosis in order to consolidate the role of social development in the overall development processes in the coming decades.

How meaningful and constructive are the actual deliberations will nevertheless depend on how well we as participants perform. The impressive professional background and caliber of delegates assembled here have given me assurance and confidence that we will surpass our expectations.

Here, I put in a vote of thanks to all those who have helped to plan and organize this meeting. To our friends and colleagues from our headquarters in Vienna, from our regional offices, from various countries where our national committees operate, and to all those who have assisted us from all corners of the world, I extend our sincere gratitude. To the Hong Kong Government and the Acting Governor of Hong Kong, we are deeply indebted for giving us valuable moral as well as financial support.

As the host city, Hong Kong has been looking forward to this XXth ICSW world conference, and we are extremely happy to see the event finally take place. Allow me, on behalf of the Conference Organizing Committee, again to extend to each and every one of you a very warm and cordial welcome. Let me assure you that your needs and comforts are very much our concern. I promise you that we will do our best to accommodate your needs and answer your calls for assistance. Hong Kong is a small place, but our people have a warm heart. We offer you our friendship and hospitality in the hope that you will want to visit us again and again.

I hope you will enjoy your stay in Hong Kong, and let us all work toward making this a successful conference.

ADDRESS

HIS EXCELLENCY SIR JACK CATER, K.B.E., J.P.

ACTING GOVERNOR OF HONG KONG

ON BEHALF of the people and the Government of Hong Kong, I have much pleasure in welcoming the officials of the ICSW, other distinguished visitors, and all participants in the XXth International Conference on Social Welfare. Hong Kong is glad to have the opportunity of hosting this important international conference, and I hope that you will not find it wanting in the arrangements that have been made for your stay here.

The theme of this conference, "Social Development in Times of Economic Uncertainty," is clearly most apt. It is particularly so against the backdrop of Hong Kong where the economy is so largely influenced by external forces quite beyond its control. Of course, we are all living in a period of great uncertainty, characterized by the specter of escalating oil prices, the threat of economic recession, political unrest in many parts of the world and—in spite of fine words to the contrary—increasingly restrictive trade attitudes and practices adopted by many major industrialized countries. These uncertainties make forward planning, whether economic or social, a hazardous exercise at best, and more so in the case of territories like this one; for in Hong Kong we must rely on the export of goods to earn our living.

Hong Kong has no "natural resources" apart from a well-situated harbor and—highly important—an industrious and versatile work force. However, very good use has been made of these resources, and we have enjoyed rapid economic growth over the last few years. It was not always thus. We have had more than our fair share of pressures and disasters during these past thirty years. There can, for example, be few communities in the world that could have withstood, overcome, and then flourished again after the harrowing period of the Pacific war, the postwar period, and the early 1950s when our population increased dramatically from 460,000 to 2.5 million: in one six-month period over 500,000 people streamed across the border into Hong Kong from China. Following that, and with the outbreak of the Korean war, our entrepôt function virtually ceased. But Hong Kong did not sit back and bemoan its fate: that is not our style. Our energies were diverted into developing our own industries, into developing our own trade. Aid from outside was minimal, our task mind-bogglingly enormous. We had to haul ourselves up by our bootstraps but first we had to make those bootstraps! Those were years of real difficulties and trials, but they led to a certain economic success which we are determined to maintain: Hong Kong is now the world's leading exporter of toys, complete watches, metal watchbands, radios, artificial flowers, torches and candles, in value or in quantity terms; and, after Italy, we are the second largest exporter of clothing in the world. We have virtually full employment, and in Asia, our wages are second only to those in Japan.

Of course, no one pretends that Hong Kong is anything like perfect—none of us is. There is an enormous amount to do and a great deal of room for improvement, but the prosperity we have achieved in recent years has enabled the government to move beyond its task of satisfying basic human needs, which had guided much of our endeavors in the 1950s and 1960s, and to seek wider improvements in our social services, our leisure and cultural amenities, and our living and working environments.

The 1970s saw significant advances in our education, health, housing, and social welfare programs. We now have nine years of free, compulsory, primary and junior secondary education; also we have an expanding, heavily subsidized, senior secondary and tertiary education system. Our general standard of health has steadily improved too. It now compares very favorably with that in the advanced industrialized countries.

Then we have our massive government housing program, which already houses over two million people, or 40 percent of the population, and this is planned to continue in growth at the rate of 15,000 new flats each year. Whole new towns are being built in the New Territories so as to provide much-needed relief for the very congested older urban areas. I am sure you will be visiting a number of these areas. The government has taken particular care in the planning of social services for these new towns in order to insure their integrated and balanced development. You can well imagine the challenge that such unique opportunities present.

In the field of social welfare we have a noncontributory social security system which insures that everyone can afford the basic necessities of life. This income-maintenance scheme is supplemented by additional allowances on a non-means-tested basis for the disabled and the elderly. In other areas, we have comprehensive plans to expand and improve services for the disabled, for the elderly, for young people, and for the preschool and primary school age groups. But in spite of all these achievements, there is—as I have said—still a very great deal more to be done, as you will see. We are very conscious that Hong Kong must not rest on its laurels. Hong Kong, in my experience, never does! It has never had the chance to! And at this time, especially, we are aware that our achievements and our aims in the field of social services are in danger of being undermined, due to the recent massive influx of immigrants from China as well as the refugees, the "boat people," from Vietnam.

The tragedy of Vietnam has, of course, been highlighted in international forums. The arrival of the boat refugees was the most dramatic and tragic event of 1979. In the first nine months some 70,000 reached Hong Kong—and how many more of these brave souls perished on the journey it is impossible to say. To our everlasting credit, we—overcrowded Hong Kong—turned none away: they were landed as transients and housed in specially erected or converted camps. No one who saw the teeming sheds where arrivals were processed, or the packed boats awaiting their turn to land, will ever forget the sight. The strain on the public services was immense, and the success of the Geneva conferences came as an enormous relief.

But when the conferences end and the delegates depart, it is all too easy for some countries not faced with the realities of coping with these vast numbers conveniently to forget the urgency that international efforts be made to resettle the refugees. Some host countries have responded magnificently, and we are grateful to them; but there are others who are rich, who have resources, who virtually prefer to turn a blind eye. We must do everything we can to keep this matter, this matter of very great urgency, in the forefront of the international conscience.

An even more intractable problem, from Hong Kong's point of view, is the greatly increased numbers of people coming here from China, both legally and illegally. In 1979 alone, 180,000 people came across our border and into this territory, which is already one of the most densely populated places on earth. As you can imagine, these additional refugees have stretched our social services to the limit and have threatened to erode the improvements we have made, so hard-won, over the past three decades. Now we have to look again at our plans for education, housing, health, and welfare provisions, and revise them to take into account this much-swollen and swelling population.

And so yet once more, Hong Kong is having to face up to an extraordinary, a seemingly impossible, problem. Hong Kong has overcome this kind of problem before, it is true, and I have no doubt will do so again; for I have the greatest possible respect and admiration for the ability of Hong Kong to overcome adversity—but it will not be easy. Meantime, and in these circumstances, we shall have a struggle to maintain, let alone to improve, the "quality of life"—which, as I have told you, for us has been so hard-won.

I hope that during your stay here you will take the opportunity to see a good deal of Hong Kong, its territory and its people, and examine its development. Your conference program is very full, I know, and there will be much to discuss. I do urge you, though, to make a little time to explore this city, the countryside (which is quite beautiful), and our lovely islands. We are unashamedly proud of our Hong Kong and are delighted to welcome all our visitors to this dynamic and exciting place.

As you get to know us, and remember the quite extraordinary numbers of people who have come here to make it their home over the years, how we have assimilated this enormous number of pretty disparate people of different backgrounds, languages, and dialects, I think you will be surprised. And when you visit China, as I understand many of you intend to do, you may well understand even more about Hong Kong.

I wish the conference great success. I trust you will renew old associations and make many new friends and especially, though, that from now on you will all be "friends of Hong Kong."

VOTE OF THANKS

INGRID GELINEK

SECRETARY-GENERAL, INTERNATIONAL COUNCIL ON SOCIAL WELFARE

PERMIT ME to start with thanking your Excellency for your gracious and warm words of welcome. On behalf of the ICSW I wish to express our gratitude for your interesting and thoughtful comments on our conference theme. They are certainly an inspiration for our forthcoming deliberations, they were most helpful and encouraging. We will approach our subject with an earnest effort and a serious desire to find—if perhaps no solution—the next step: the next step in the forever unending human search for increased well-being, for more individual happiness, for an improved human condition in the communities, societies, and countries on our earth.

The opening of a world gathering is always a solemn occasion, and all of us here face the challenge inherent in any international meeting. Our knowledge of participation in an international assembly leads to questions which should be raised, particularly at such a moment: Are we really able and willing to bridge the gaps between different cultures and value patterns, between different languages and different conceptions in the approach to welfare? Are we sufficiently flexible, tolerant, and patient to learn from one another, to listen to one another? Do we have sufficient interest and capacity to build with great care and sensitivity relationships with our colleagues from other parts of the world? Do we have the strength to break the isolation in which so many of us work?

Not only do we realize the challenges of international meetings, we also have a great deal of experience in many areas of social welfare. Sometimes it seems that we are so overinvolved in our activities, that we know so much, that we have lost sight of what we are really talking about: social welfare or social action or social service or social development or—perhaps about yet another concept, which so far we have been unable to define adequately.

And, at least if we are honest, we have to raise the questions, Are the people interested in our language problems and our struggles to define issues? Do they understand us? Or is it not so that all they want are opportunities to participate in assistance programs which would result in better chances, in more social justice for the needy, the underprivileged, the marginal groups, wherever they may be on this earth?

In this context, as responsible human beings, we also have to raise the issue of our own competence. Are we really effective, and not just routine, interpreters of human suffering? Are we caring, and not only paid, advocates of the disadvantaged? Are we sufficiently qualified and sufficiently informed to be designers of adequate and need-oriented programs? Are we willing to accept the risks inherent in decisions and actions which touch upon the life of human beings?

At this moment many uncertainties confront us, besides the economic uncertainty spelled out in our conference theme. It will not be easy to solve them. But the need to face questions, the desire to find answers, is of paramount importance to an international conference. During the coming days participants can reflect together on common issues. During the coming week professionals, colleagues, can meet with the chance of getting to know one another as human beings.

Some days ago, in our ICSW business meetings, the remark was made: "Information can be obtained through computer networks these days. But never will this replace the profound quality, the rich and exciting reality of knowledge obtained when human beings from different parts of the world meet face to face." This will be possible in the next week, because of our many, many supporters, colleagues, and friends in Hong Kong.

We owe deep gratitude to the Government of Hong Kong for all its support and financial assistance, which was absolutely vital to enable us to organize this conference.

We thank the president and the governing bodies of the Hong Kong Council of Social Service and especially also the staff of the Council for their untiring efforts over and above their normal work.

We thank Y. F. Hui, Director of the Hong Kong Council of Social Service, under whose leadership the Conference Organizing Committee planned and executed the numberless actions required to assure the smooth running of such a complex meeting.

Our special thanks go to Winnifred Mary Ng, the Conference Secretary, and her staff, for constant, effective, and highly competent work.

Many hundreds of volunteers have been involved in the preparations for this conference. In many subgroups and at all levels they have given and will continue to give freely their time, their skills, their resources, their inspirations. All of us owe deep gratitude to these invaluable collaborators.

Also, in the name of the ICSW I pay tribute to two people whose professional assistance made the development of the conference program possible: Harold Ho, chairman of the International Program Committee, and James R. Dumpson, the world rapporteur.

The conference program should be considered as a framework for constructive discussions on a challenging theme and for manifold and rich human contacts. On this basis we are looking forward to an exciting and stimulating week.

*Social Development in Times
of Economic Uncertainty*

Conference Working Document

SOCIAL DEVELOPMENT IN TIMES OF ECONOMIC UNCERTAINTY

JAMES R. DUMPSON

ASSISTANT DIRECTOR, NEW YORK COMMUNITY TRUST, UNITED STATES

THE PREPARATION of a basic working document, a "world report" related to the theme of the conference, was initiated by the Program Committee of the 1978 Jerusalem conference. A world report was determined to be useful for providing a summarized overview of issues related to the conference discussions for participants who represent a variety of cultural, social, political, and economic backgrounds. The Program Committee for the XXth International Conference again authorized a world report. The president of the ICSW appointed the author of this report as the world rapporteur. Each of the five regions of the ICSW was asked to appoint a regional rapporteur to synthesize reports from each country in the region and to forward a regional report to the world rapporteur. To assist in the preparation of regional reports, I prepared an outline for each regional rapporteur. This guide was based on the development of the conference theme, and the discussion outline by the Program Committee for the small discussion groups at the conference.

Unfortunately, the timetable for submission of the regional reports was not adhered to, and the variations of content and organization of the regional reports, while understandable, presented difficult problems in achieving a high degree of coherence and unity in the finalization of the report. However, excerpts and footnoted material have been used selectively when recasting or attempting to rewrite a sentence or paragraph risked loss of authenticity. The deadline of the Hong Kong Conference Organizing Committee for receipt of the report, for reproduction in time for registration at the conference, prevented any consultation with regional rapporteurs after their reports were received.

The author is grateful to the regional rapporteurs for their careful preparatory work which, I am sure, experienced similar difficulties as they related to access to their country reports:

    Africa   J.A. Ahouzi, Director of Social Affairs, Government of the Republic of the Ivory Coast

    Asia and the West Pacific   Lawrance H. Thompson, Secretary, Japanese National Committee, ICSW

    Europe   Adrian C.M. De Kok, Ministry of Cultural Affairs, Recreation, and Social Welfare, Netherlands

    Latin America   M. Agusta de Luna Albano, Social Worker, Rio de Janeiro, Brazil

    North America   H. Philip Hepworth, Associate Professor, University of Regina, Regina, Canada

This report could not have been completed without the valuable assistance of three colleagues of the author. The world rapporteur is grateful to Edward J. Mullen, University of Chicago, for the insightful and scholarly organization and interpretation of the world development indicators, the content of which I have incorporated in the report; to Steve Moisoff, the Greater New York Fund/United Way, and Michael Dowling, Fordham University, both of whom reviewed and summarized selected reference material which I have incorporated in my synthesis of the regional reports.

OVERVIEW

Economic development and social development are mutually dependent. Yet, most industrialized nations are entering the 1980s in a state of economic uncertainty, and most less developed countries are beginning the decade in an economically precarious state with little hope for improvement. Does this mean that social progress need be temporarily suspended?

What it is certain to mean is that the choice of social welfare programs will increasingly entail a careful and conscious trade-off between what is desirable and what is affordable. It will be as much a moral decision as an economic or social one. And it will not be easy.

For the "have" nations of the world, forty years of taken-for-granted prosperity have brought about a greater degree of social awareness, improved knowledge of social conditions, and increased familiarity with a diversity of life styles. Prosperity has brought about a proliferation of social programs and a number of variations on the welfare state. It has not, however, provided these governments with the experience required for balancing competing societal interests. It seemed as though they could all have guns and butter.

Present economic realities, such as fiscal crises, necessitate major reevaluation of expensive social welfare projects and priorities. The role of the state in providing these programs has, however, become so institutionalized that any cutbacks will be politically unpopular, socially costly, and perhaps even morally unjustifiable. And yet, one must ask whether there are domains in which state intervention is no longer justified, and whether the centralized and sometimes dehumanized welfare bureaucracies which have evolved might serve their clients better as local, decentralized units.

The twin pillars of inflation and unemployment—long the bane of developing countries—have increased to serious proportions in most of North America and Western Europe, though they are still relatively manageable compared with the situation in some other countries. But as governments attempt to bring these conditions under control, money continues to become tighter. In all countries, therefore, the primary issue is the availability and distribution of resources. With the economic growth rate for the 1980s projected at zero or minus one for the OECD (Organization for Economic Cooperation and Development) countries, and still less for others, individual wages and public budgets—including social welfare benefits—will certainly suffer the consequences. And since most social budgets are committed to economically disadvantaged people, the question becomes how to decrease expenditures without further disadvantaging these most vulnerable groups—and how to accomplish this in a socially acceptable fashion.

The ICSW, for administrative and program convenience, has divided the world into five regions: Africa, Asia and Western Pacific, Europe, Middle East and Mediterranean Area, Latin America and the Caribbean, North America. Regional differences, and country differences within regions, can be enormous, impeding the impulse toward facile generalizations. Levels of social development vary as much as, if not more than, economic indicators. To take Asia as just one example, the countries of the region represent a great range of economic productivity. Per capita gross national product (GNP) statistics show that Afghanistan, India, Indonesia, Nepal, Pakistan, and Sri Lanka are all in the low range, with under $200 income per person per year. Australia, Japan, and New Zealand are in the extremely high range, with an annual per capita income of between $4,000 and $6,000.

Economic global interdependence has brought about a new range of shared experiences and postindustrial trends which are fairly universal, and which have significant economic impacts. Among these are:

1. Great structural unemployment, increasing with automation and threatening particularly youth
2. Increasing amounts of leisure time unfilled with meaningful or productive activities
3. Increasing numbers of aged people; population growing older and a "graying" of populations in many countries
4. Increasingly diverse life styles, such as single-parent families, divorce, open marriages
5. Emerging role of women outside the home
6. Influx and use of foreign migrant workers
7. Proliferation of welfare state bureaucracies
8. Degeneration of the ideal of equality and equity in stressful economic times.

These trends reflect the consequences (both desirable and undesirable) of industrialized life. Having identified them, governments are seeking ways to mitigate their effects. The result has been the development of comprehensive social welfare programs to provide various types of universal benefits, such as social security. Some would now argue that the allocation of these benefits can no longer be universally available but must be restricted to groups defined as having special needs. Others, however, argue that even in a time of prosperity, the provision of certain services, such as health care, has been neither adequate nor universally available and accessible.

Yet, the fact of social progress on a global scale cannot be seriously disputed. It has, however, been based on economic prosperity. The uncertainty of the continuation of economic conditions in almost all regions of the world places provision of social supports in jeopardy and raises the question: Who gets what?

The United States and Canada are still manifestly wealthy, more so than most countries of the world. Their peoples are highly favored. At the same time, this prosperity is not equitably shared, whether on a personal, sexual, racial, ethnic, age-related, or regional basis. The economically and socially underdeveloped areas of both countries pose a continuing threat to the well-being of each.

In Western Europe, the postwar material progress has not been matched by an increased sense of well-being and personal happiness.

In Africa, especially in the non-oil-producing countries, the slowing down of the economy in the industrialized countries has gravely affected the economy of the primary producing countries, particularly those which have an annual income of less than $400 per inhabitant. Imports are then no longer covered by exports, and this results in poor economic growth and an exacerbation of economic uncertainty.

In Latin America and the Caribbean countries, the long-term forecast is similarly discouraging, primarily for countries at the lower income levels. Even without well-documented knowledge about the interaction between social and economic factors, the prospects for millions of people is for a life characterized by malnutrition, illiteracy, disease, high infant mortality rates, and low life expectancies, none of which corresponds to any reasonable definition of human dignity and well-being.

In Asia and the Pacific, uncertainty and disillusionment characterize current attitudes toward development. India's Sugata Dasgupta has suggested a "redistribution of poverty" since there are clearly insufficient resources available in the world to make the "redistribution of wealth" a viable proposition.

The concept of social development[1] as an international obligation became institutionalized in 1961 with the first United Nations Development Decade. Social development traditionally discussed in terms of a microperspective (growth within the family system) is today discussed in macro terms. It is now used in the broad context of individual, organizational, institutional, and societal change, from both a national and an international perspective. The basis for the growing interest in social development as a measure of well-being arises from four interrelated sources.

1. The failure of economic development alone in the less developed countries to raise substantially the living standard of the majority of the population
2. The failure in the advanced countries to cope satisfactorily with the social dysfunctions created by economic success and growth, such as urbanization, impersonalization, environmental hazards, and so forth
3. The relatively poor record of traditional social welfare initiatives in substantially rejuvenating the human condition
4. The need to see human beings as the subject of development rather than its object.

Since the concept of social development must be viewed in relation to the developed as well as the developing and underdeveloped countries, all of which have their unique historical, cultural, social, economic, and ideological characteristics, any

---

[1] See J. F. X. Paiva, "A Conception of Social Development," *Social Service Review* (June 1977), pp. 327–34.

definition of "social" must be broad in nature. Paiva gives us such a definition:

The goal and substance of social development is the welfare of the people, as determined by the people themselves and the consequent creation or alteration of institutions so as to create a capacity for meeting human needs at all levels and for improving the quality of human relationships between people and societal institutions.

Social development is based on the belief that human needs and aspirations are important in facilitating an improved social order. Welfare and happiness cannot be measured by levels of income alone, but also by levels of social justice and equity. Human beings, in their totality, are the central focus of concern. As the Economic Commission for Asia and the Far East Resolution 99 of 1969 declared: "Development is an integrated and balanced process in which social progress is no longer regarded as an appendage of economic growth but rather as a factor that to a large extent conditions economic growth."

It seems safe to state that the ideal has not been realized. Neither the good intentions of the industrialized countries nor the best efforts of the developing countries have been sufficient to bring about full realization of the developmental process. The basic prerequisites of sound social development have in many instances been neglected or forgotten: political will (the official commitment to the concept for social development, with all its characteristics), ideology, and cooperation. Many development efforts have failed to bring about improvement in the standard of living or the quality of life of people in both the developed and the developing countries because of the inequitable distribution of opportunities and resources within and among countries. For social development efforts to succeed, four basic ingredients must be in place:

Socioeconomic integration. The relevant components of the social and the economic institutions must be unified in one comprehensive strategy.

Structural change. Structural changes that improve the opportunity for resource allocation and distribution. Continued growth in the GNP without such structural change will not result in the improvement of the well-being of the majority of a population.

Institutional development. Structural change needs to be accompanied by the development of new institutions, the modification of existing ones or the elimination of dysfunctional ones. Otherwise, the status quo will absorb, in time, efforts at change.

Institutional renewal. Constant evaluation in institutional structure is necessary in order to protect against obsolescence.

The essential point to be made in consideration of social development is the well-being of people. They are, as Paiva points out, "the true subjects of development." Efforts must be focused on improving the inherent capacity of people, allowing them to realize their full potential while at the same time altering those societal institutions that hinder the achievement of such goals. At a time of economic uncertainty this task becomes all the more crucial and difficult. For large parts of the world, economic uncertainty is a way of life. For most of the Western nations, especially the United States and Canada, the uncertainty presents unfamiliar challenges that they are only minimally prepared to meet. Increasingly there is tension between emphasis on efficiency and productivity at the expense of meaningful concern for human rights and human well-being.

According to several recent studies, however, alternatives are not absolutely necessary. With a reordering of priorities, available resources are sufficient to continue to provide social benefits to those who need them. The World Bank, for example, estimates that the dollar cost of eliminating poverty over a ten-year period would be about $125 billion. A study by the Brookings Institution reached a similarly optimistic conclusion in terms of eliminating hunger and malnutrition; and UNESCO has calculated the possibility of reducing illiteracy by two-thirds, at a cost of less than $2 billion over a ten-year period.

Efforts to integrate and systematize development policy at all levels will unquestionably have to focus on the rural populations who live at or near the poverty level in towns and villages all over the world. They do not own land, they do not have enough to eat or drink, often not even clean water. They are not in good health, they are weak, undereducated, and inexperienced.

In the future, Western democracies will have to help alleviate these problems of absolute poverty without encouraging the emergence of dictatorships. The welfare systems of all nations will have to reorder their priorities to allow available resources to be used more discretely, that is, by targeting local resources to meet local needs through local decision-making processes. By developing pride in participation rather than in possession, the mutually dependent goals of economic growth and social development should continue to flourish, even amid economic uncertainty.

HISTORICAL, POLITICAL, AND CULTURAL FACTORS

The debate over social development is probably taking place in every country of the world, but the definition of the term no doubt varies greatly from state to state. The perception is influenced as much by cultural and historical factors as by economic and political ones. Obviously, these differ significantly.

There is a common perception, however, that social programs are essential, so that even modest reductions in welfare outlays are universally unpopular. Even in affluent Canada, for example, relatively small cuts in the country's social programs reportedly contributed to the overthrow first of the Liberal government and later of the new Conservative government. Social programs are designed to help assure a determined standard of living; people resist government actions that adversely affect social development. However defined, social development involves a subjective ordering of priorities based on societal values and interests. No country has a right to assume that its way of doing things is right and that of other countries is wrong.

In Africa the term includes all comprehensive measures taken to influence income distribution and redistribution; the objective is to offer everyone equal access to equal opportunities. For most African nations, protective social programs became necessary only when the traditional economic systems were modernized; new economic structures brought new social structures into existence. Although different countries in Africa have very different political and historical backgrounds, they often have identical social needs. Consequently, over the past decade most African nations have concentrated their social development policies on regional development, education, housing, and employment. But certain regions have had to address special problems which impede development, primarily the unfavorable climatic conditions which have caused drought in Ethiopia and the Sahel area, and the invasions of migrant locusts which have ruined crops throughout East Africa. The resulting decline in agricultural production has meant severe food shortages and other hardships for Africa's largely rural population. And experience has shown that social development, however defined, tends not to flourish amid economic deprivation.

The countries of Latin America and the Caribbean factor entirely different cultural and historical experiences into their perception of social development. Some of the social-cultural observations put forth at the 1979 Economic Commission for Latin America (CEPAL) conference in Mexico include the following:

> The Latin American has an innate bent to welcome people, to share with others, to live in fraternal charity and unselfishness. . . . He has a clear awareness of his own dignity, of his desire to be politically and socially involved. Community organizations are widespread, there are many cooperative movements among the common people. There is a respect for the originality of native cultures and communities and a deep love of homeland.

This innate sense of individual worth, as well as the belief in regional solidarity, has implications for the kind of programs which Latin American governments have devised to achieve social progress.

In every country in Asia, without exception, the family is viewed as the focal point for realizing social development: There is concern among some social analysts that the family in Western industrial countries is disintegrating. At the ICSW regional meeting held in Australia in August, 1979, the government of Indonesia stated a commonly held precept that "children constitute an integral and inseparable part of the family as an entity. It will therefore be impossible to separate activities for materializing child welfare from activities for materializing the welfare of the family." Even in the now thoroughly industrialized country of Japan, the extended family is still predominant—70 percent of those over age sixty-five live with their adult children. Japanese government planners recognize that the family will have to be considered an important factor in developing systems of community services for the future.

In Western Europe the concept of social development varies markedly from country to country. The United Kingdom emphasizes the socioeconomic element of development; that is, there is the belief that the government's economic and industrial policies will significantly affect the level and direction of social progress. For Austrians, social development quite simply means full employment. Because of the nation's own past history—in 1918-34 unemployment was one of the key reasons leading to the breakdown of democracy—a great deal of public spending has gone toward creating jobs and helping people to keep them. In Switzerland, on the other hand, where there are no structural economic problems such as unemployment, social development is directed toward the general well-being, especially of the weakest groups in the population. In Denmark, Finland, Norway, and Sweden as well as in the Netherlands, the concept of social development is incorporated into the very fabric of the welfare state. The highest public expenditures in the world—67 percent and 60 percent respectively of national income—are in Sweden and the Netherlands.

The small and politically turbulent nation of Cyprus perceives social development quite differently from most other countries in the world. As a result of the Turkish invasion in 1974, one third of the population was displaced from its homes; 40 percent of the nation's territory was occupied by a foreign power; and thousands of Cypriots were killed, orphaned, or otherwise affected by this disastrous event. The concept and process of social development in Cyprus, therefore, have taken the form of reconstruction, with a view toward alleviating the human suffering caused by war. Social policies seek to secure the physical survival of the thousands of families who were uprooted, and to reintegrate social groups and communities. Clearly, housing has had a very high priority.

In North America, social development is again based on very different life experiences. It can be argued that poverty in that part of the world is only relative. Nonetheless, it is persistent. Poverty is a structural feature of North American society, a function of the maldistribution of resources and, for many, of opportunities. There are poorer countries which distribute their resources in such a way that they do not experience the same degree of poverty found in parts of North America. In terms of relevant economic and social indicators, they score higher. In the United States and Canada, development policies seek to improve the standard of living of all levels of society, but they are unclear as to what level of poverty is considered tolerable. Conversely, there seems to be some difficulty in setting a limit on the degree of affluence which is desirable. These and other problems notwithstanding, it seems that the North American perception of social progress is still informed by the democratic, egalitarian ideals with which these countries began their existence.

The individual experiences of the nations of the world cannot easily be collectivized into one tidy conceptual phenomenon in so far as social development is concerned. The elements of development which are indeed globally applicable, however, have to do with the fact that economic indicators are by themselves no longer adequate determinants of progress. Much less quantifiable factors—the quality of life, for example—have come to be of equal importance. The production of goods and raw materials is neither more nor less important than their distribution. Social development is now recognized as an integrated process whose primary focus must be on the human factor.

ECONOMIC REALITIES AND UNCERTAINTIES

The most important factor leading to the present economic situation has been the rising cost of oil. Higher and higher energy prices have had an adverse impact on every oil-importing nation, while the increasingly affluent oil-producing countries have contributed to a worsening of international relations.

The most immediate consequences of this phenomenon have, of course, been economic ones. Even in North America, frequently characterized as the epitome of a capitalist society, the automobile industry which has long been a predominant force in the United States economy has run into serious financial difficulties; the government has had to intervene, so far, to bail out one major auto manufacturer. In the United Kingdom as well, the steel and car industries are announcing widescale redundancies, and the Conservative government elected in May, 1979, is seeking to reduce public expenditures by deep cuts in all areas except defense and law and order.

Many of the Latin American countries which depend primarily on exports (including oil) are facing tremendous economic difficulties. Of their twelve basic exports, just four—cocoa, coffee, tin, and oil—experienced price increases in the 1970s. The actual prices of others, including sugar, copper, soya, bananas, and iron ore, all of which are relevant to different economies throughout the region, declined dramatically over the ten-year period, in some cases corresponding to 50 percent of 1970 prices.

Despite a stronger capacity developed by Latin American countries to defend themselves against harsh international situations, there is no doubt that the slow and unstable expansion of the industrial centers since 1974 has had an unfavorable effect on the region's development possibilities.

In Brazil, 1979 saw, for the first time in the country's history, a situation where total oil imports plus interest and amortization of the external debt exceeded the export value. With interest plus amortization totaling $10.2 billion and oil imports not exceeding $6.2 billion, the total amount of $16.7 billion represents 11 percent above the expected $15 billion value of exports.

These data mean that the Brazilian economy has become, in its balance of payments, extremely vulnerable to the international economic evolution. Any increase in oil prices will tend to raise the cost of the country's imports, to spread world inflation, to restrain any slowdown in international interest rates to which 70 percent of the external debt is subject, and to encourage a climate of economic protectionism capable of hindering the expansion of the Brazilian exports to the industrialized nations. In spite of Brazil's sustained efforts to further the growth of oil substitutes in order to promote the use of hydroelectric power plants and alcohol production, in addition to an anti-inflation program not detrimental to the country's development, the impact of international conditions is seriously impairing implementation of certain social programs, among which the one referring to "wage policy" is, obviously, of crucial importance.

According to studies carried out by CEPAL, 40 percent of Latin American families were living under poverty conditions in 1979. This means that more than 110 million people could not get the minimum amount of goods indispensable to meeting their basic needs. In turn, 20 percent of families lived in a state of indigence (total deprivation); that is to say, they lacked the minimum resources necessary even for survival.

To many informed observers the problem of poverty in the Latin American region is becoming alarming, not only because it is widespread, but also due to the unsatisfactory manner in which it is being attacked. During the 1960s and early 1970s the absolute number of poor people remained constant, while their proportion of the total population decreased approximately from 50 percent to 40 percent.

A study conducted by CEPAL on the situation in nine Latin American countries reports that the percentage of the total population living in conditions of poverty in 1970 was as follows: below 10 percent in Argentina; between 10 percent and 25 percent in Costa Rica, Chile, and Venezuela; between 25 percent and 40 percent in Mexico; between 40 percent and 55 percent in Brazil, Colombia, and Peru; and above 55 percent in Honduras. It is, however, probable, owing to the deterioration of the Latin American economic growth rate over the past recent years, that the number of poor families in the region has now increased.

An analysis of the characteristics of poor families reveals that rural families are affected by poverty to a much greater extent than urban families: 62 percent of the former and 26 percent of the latter of the total number of cases examined. Other analyses indicate that the lower the family income level, the higher the dependency on work earnings. They also show that there is a close relationship between unemployment and poverty: although most of the heads of indigent and poor families have some employment, a high percentage are underemployed. It is worth mentioning that, according to studies made by the International Labor Organization (ILO) and CEPAL in Latin America, unemployment affects 5 percent of the labor force, while underemployment affects about 30 percent.

In respect to personal employment characteristics of family heads, it is found that educational level is one of the variables having stronger correlation with poverty levels: most of the heads of indigent and poor families have had three years or less of basic education.

It should be added that the nearly nonexistent organizational power of the poor prevents them from any effective involvement in the determination of policies and programs that affect their lives. If present economic conditions are maintained, it can be said with a high degree of certainty that the living standards of deprived sectors of the population will not be raised to acceptable levels in the foreseeable future.

For the OECD countries, the rate of economic growth as of February, 1980, was much lower than expected, due also to the sharp rises in energy and oil prices. Indeed, the economic outlook is very somber for the entire decade. In the European Economic Community, unemployment increased in all countries (except Austria and Switzerland), especially among young people, women, the poorly educated, and foreign migrant workers. Inflation in the OECD countries will go to 10 percent in 1980.

A look at the economic prospects for one OECD country which is in a relatively good fiscal situation might be revealing. The economic position of Austria was described in the European regional report. Economic uncertainties as outlined in the report cannot be projected, but certain indicators are being watched closely:

1. The future price of oil: Austria does have a little oil of its own, but is in no way able to meet its demands; in the energy sector there are also large imports of coal.

2. One of the major sources of income in Austria is tourism. In the annual service balance Austria always has a big surplus due to tourism; this depends, of course, largely on the economic situation in other countries—in other words, on how many people come to Austria for their holidays.

3. The balance of trade is important: imports will decline and exports increase again.

Exports are very closely linked to the situation on the money market. Austria is one of the "hard currency countries"; while this is important in the sense that its currency stays in line with the currencies of its principal trading partners (Germany, Switzerland), it is often very hard on exporters who have been outpriced in certain areas due to the devaluation of the dollar and, to a lesser extent, of the British pound sterling.

So while on the whole there is no cause for alarm so far as the Austrian economy is concerned, there are certain indicators to be watched. There will almost certainly be a trend to economize in public expenditures as well as in the private sector, but unless there are dramatic changes in the world situation, the Austrian economy should continue to develop at its current pace.

ASIA AND WESTERN PACIFIC

Asia represents a great range in economic productivity. In terms of the gross domestic product (GDP), Afghanistan,

Bangladesh, Burma, Cambodia, Fiji, Laos, Nepal, Singapore, Sri Lanka, and Vietnam fall in the low grouping, with less than $10 billion per year. Hong Kong, Malaysia, New Zealand, Pakistan, Taiwan, the Philippines, and Thailand fall in a middle grouping of countries that produce between $10 and $20 billion per year. Indonesia and Korea make up a kind of mid-high group with $30 to $40 billion per year. High-productivity countries include Australia, India, Iran—all between $65 and $90 billion per year. The People's Republic of China at $170 billion and Japan at $562 billion represent two independent categories. Japan just edges out the USSR as the second most productive country in the world but is still far behind the United States, which has a production of $1,872.5 billion per year.

The picture changes considerably, however, when production is related to size of population. The per capita GNP statistics would group together Afghanistan, India, Indonesia, Nepal, Pakistan, and Sri Lanka, all in the low range of under $200 per year per person. With two countries, the Philippines and Thailand, in a kind of low-middle range of $350 to $400 and Fiji, Korea, Malaysia, and Taiwan in a mid-range of roughly $700 to $1,200, the high range of $2,000 to $2,700 would include Hong Kong, Iran, and Singapore. Australia, Japan, and New Zealand constitute a kind of extra-high category of production, between $4,000 to $6,000 per year per person.

The oil crisis of October 1973, and the second oil crisis related to the fall of the Pahlevi regime in Iran in 1979 are increasingly seen as the basic date lines from which the ability of a given country to cope with economic fluctuation is measured. Charts of consumer prices for the years 1970 to the present show tremendous economic upheaval in almost every Asian country in 1974, followed by fairly stable recovery trends between 1975 and 1978. While some countries experienced a second crisis in 1979, there is as yet no sharp upsurge of the inflation trend following the most recent crisis. This indicates a general belt tightening and new sophistication in dealing with economic emergency. Actually, with the exception of the Philippines and Sri Lanka, most Asian countries suffer less now from consumer price increases than they did in 1973. For special reasons, Bangladesh and Burma suffered least. However, the Iranian hostage situation beginning in October of 1979 and the Russian invasion of Afghanistan in December of the same year have added a new note of uncertainty which does not augur well for the future.

The statistics on unemployment are spotty with much unemployment or underemployment concealed within Asia's vast rural population. Of concern are the constantly increasing unemployed, coupled with the assurance that with a constantly increasing population, vast numbers of new jobs will be required as far into the future as we can see. Australia has been particularly worried about this situation in which aggregate unemployment has risen from a negligible ratio of the working population to a current level of about 6 percent and where the ratio is as high as 25 percent among out-of-school, unskilled youth.

NORTH AMERICA

In North America the fiscal effects of the oil price increases have in most cases been more direct than the social consequences. Much of North American society has failed to change as rapidly as world economic conditions would justify: by trying to maintain an acceptable standard of living these governments have only added to the ever-mounting inflationary pressures. The excessive provision and consumption of goods and services in industrial societies have, according to some observers, brought excessive provision and consumption of welfare benefits as well. The crisis comes when resource restraints force a disruption of this system. Or, the crisis comes because of the still glaring inadequacies apparent in present social security programs. The question, then, is whether or not it is feasible to improve and extend these programs in times of economic insecurity.

The expanding federal role in both the United States and Canada in the social policy field finally became a "slave to limit" in the 1970s. The fiscal coffers were no longer bottomless. For both political and economic reasons President Nixon sought some control on federal spending. He sought also to place more responsibility for program initiation at the state and local level. The 1970s also saw an assertion of provincial autonomy in Canada. The beginning of the 1980s provides, therefore, a very good opportunity for an appraisal of an era of social policy development in the United States and Canada, which may now be in a period of rapid transition.

SOCIAL PROGRAMS IN TIMES OF ECONOMIC UNCERTAINTY

At present every country in the world has programs devised to assist the most vulnerable groups of the population. Three of the five regional reports deal with effects of economic uncertainty on social programs. A variety of areas—health, unemployment, housing, and so on—and a variety of geographic and economic contexts are covered in the three reports.

ASIA

Housing is a critical problem. The ILO's minimum target levels for world housing are 5.25 square meters per person in Africa and Asia and 7.5 square meters in Latin America. The United Nations defines overcrowding as the situation when three or more persons live in a single room. In Asia, the worst conditions exist in Pakistan, with 60.5 percent of the population living in circumstances exceeding the three-to-a-room standard; in Iran, with 46.5 percent; in Korea, with 46.6 percent; and in Sri Lanka, with 47.7 percent.

Adequate housing in Asia is reported only in Australia, New Zealand, Japan, Hong Kong, and Singapore. Hong Kong, with an advanced housing development program, still needs new housing for 1.5 million people in the decade 1972–82 to meet its goal of "self-contained housing units for every family." By mid 1979 only one third of this goal had been reached.

The per capita production of food in Asia, according to the Food and Agriculture Organization, decreased in 1970–74, even though total production increased, highlighting the population explosion aspects of the problem. Other projections indicate that whereas many developing countries have not increased food production to match economic growth, food production by 2010 will increase slightly faster than population increases. However, without fundamental development of infrastructures, it will be impossible to distribute these available resources. Developing areas will need to emphasize self-support food production, and not dependency on distribution systems. In Asian areas, access to "adequate" water is reported as being enjoyed by 50 percent to 60 percent of the population in urban areas but by only 20 percent to 30 percent in rural areas.

The pressure of population increase on health services is dramatically demonstrated in Thailand. There, the number of physicians will need to be increased from 3,230 to 14,380, other health workers from 17,740 to 91,240, and hospital beds from 33,010 to 167,470 between 1970 and the year 2000, just to maintain present standards of service.

The Asian report states that making an opportunity for education available to everyone is an essential means of preventing poverty from being transferred indefinitely from one generation to the next. Figures on expenditures indicate that a good number, ten of the twenty-three countries listed, spent between 14 percent and 22 percent of their public expenditure on education. Australia, Fiji, Japan, Korea, New Zealand, and Taiwan had between 66 percent and 78 percent of young people from five to nineteen years of age enrolled in school. On the other hand, Afghanistan, Bangladesh, Indonesia, Laos, and Pakistan had one third or less of the same age grouping in school, and there was a tremendous range of teacher/student ratio, from 258 students to one teacher in Afghanistan to 25 to one in Australia.

Asia has a 33 percent illiteracy rate, quite comparable to the world average of 27 percent. However, fifteen of the twenty-three countries listed exceed the Asian average, and Afghanistan, Bangladesh, Iran, Laos, Nepal, and Pakistan each have illiteracy rates in excess of 70 percent. Perhaps the most startling fact revealed very clearly in the data is the flagrant sexual bias toward greater education opportunity for males than for females. The very worst example is Japan, where illiteracy as such is practically nonexistent, probably confined to handicapped individuals who, until 1979, were not eligible for compulsory education. Even under these rather ideal circumstances, however, the illiteracy rate for women was some three times higher than that for men.

By 1985 school enrollment is expected to increase considerably. India, for instance, is putting a great deal of effort into education. However, with population increases, the number of children not enrolled will also increase. Major problems involved in this situation are that schools are concentrated in urban areas, they tend to focus on curricula leading to prestigious higher education, they do not take into consideration the practical needs and interests of the students. There is a resulting high rate of dropout. The great need is for functional, widely dispersed, low-cost educational programs, including due emphasis on adult education programs.

The unemployment statistics for Asia, while showing steady increases in numbers, do not reveal the full significance of the problem. Much of the difficulty is concentrated among the vast numbers of rural underemployed individuals. Since there are no unemployment benefit programs in all but two or three Asian countries, even underemployment leads very quickly to absolute poverty.

The problem can be attributed only partially to lack of aggregate economic growth. Largely, it represents bias in favor of capital-intensive labor rather than labor-intensive small industry and rural development. The world work force is expected to grow 2.7 percent per year to the year 2000. Full employment at that point will require one billion new jobs in the nonsocialist and 600 million new jobs in the socialist world.

THE UNITED STATES AND CANADA

There is growing concern with the general growth of government intervention and with the growth of government itself.

There is concern with the effect of major social, economic, and demographic trends. There is concern, also, with provisions made, provisions not made, goals achieved, and goals not achieved. Both countries are dealing with economic uncertainty rather than with economic catastrophe, with declining rates of growth rather than with massive cutbacks.

The demographic character of both the United States and Canada is in many ways highly similar; this fact has particular relevance for two vulnerable groups, young people and women. In both countries there was a peaking of the birth rate and the number of births in the late 1950s; this is reflected in several ways in the late 1970s and early 1980. There is a bulge of young people completing their education and moving into the work force. At the same time, more women are entering the labor force either after early completion of their families, or before marriage and then staying in employment during marriage and even while they have young children.

Over several decades the labor force participation of men and women has gradually converged. We now have a situation in both countries where slightly less than 80 percent of men and about 50 percent of women are working. All age groups of women, but especially those in the child-bearing years, are involved in this increased participation.

But while women increasingly enter and stay in paid employment, they still do not earn incomes comparable to those of men. In the mid-1970s in the United States women in full-time work earned $6,828 compared with $12,465 (in 1977 dollars) earned by men. The median money income of women at $8,814 (black $8,290; white $8,870) compared with $15,070 for men.

The special case of single-parent families illustrates further some of the social and economic disadvantages experienced by women. In 1977 there were 1,500,000 male-headed, single-parent families compared to 7,713,000 female-headed, single-parent families in the United States. Over two thirds of the male-headed families had no children under the age of eighteen, whereas almost two thirds of the female-headed families did have such children to care for. Twelve percent of white children under eighteen were cared for only by their mother, and 42 percent of black children. Some 50 percent of these female-headed (black, white, and other) families with children were below the poverty level, and a further 10 percent were less than 25 percent above the poverty level.

The situation in Canada is very similar to that in the United States. In 1976 there were almost five times as many single-parent families with female heads (464,350) as with male heads (94,990). Over 80 percent had offspring under the age of twenty-five, and 54 percent had at least one child under the age of fifteen. Of 195,000 single-parent families judged to be poor in 1977, 83 percent had at least one child under the age of sixteen. These families are predominantly female-headed.

In 1976 divorce accounted for 21 percent of female-led, single-parent families compared with only 6 percent in 1966; at the same time, widowhood was responsible for 42 percent of female-led families in 1976 compared with 62 percent in 1966. There have thus been some major social changes in a short period of time.

Whereas 7 percent of all families were female-headed, single-parent families in 1977, this type of family accounted for 20 percent of families in the lowest income quintile. In fact, since 1967 there appears despite some fluctuations to have been a concentration of this group in the lowest quintile.

The proportion of income received by low-income single-parent families from government transfer payments increased from 56 percent in 1967 to 74 percent in 1977. Income assistance accounted for two thirds of these payments. This presents a serious problem in Canada. The same appears to be true in the United States with its Aid to Families with Dependent Children program, in which a large proportion of low-income families are dependent for most of their income on the most stigmatized assistance programs.

The 1970s marked the coming of age of the baby boom which peaked in the late 1950s. The education system grew as the child population grew, and continued growing as the child population grew older. As births fell, so in due course enrollments in the lower grades fell, and this phenomenon has gradually passed through the school system. Universities flourished as their own enrollments grew and as even higher enrollments were expected. But in the face of economic uncertainties and some doubts about the benefits of higher education, universities in the late 1970s and early 1980s have not experienced the record enrollments which demographically might have been predicted.

School enrollments (for ages 5–34) rose by some 28 percent between 1960 and 1970 in the United States. Since 1970 there has been a slight decline, offset in some measure by the inclusion of three- and four-year-old children in nursery schools, but the overall level of enrollment has remained about 60 million (50 million white and 10 million black and other) each year.

The Canadian education system shows the same "maturing" tendencies as the American education system. In 1972, 82 percent of people over 14 years of age had secondary education or less; by 1985 it is projected this figure will have fallen to 68 percent. In terms of people leaving school, by 1985 over 50 percent will have some postsecondary education, and 34 percent will have completed this stage of their education. By 1975, 42 percent of full-time, postsecondary students and 51 percent of part-time students were women (compared with 39 percent in 1962).

By way of contrast only 2.4 percent of registered Indians in Canada receiving education were enrolled in universities, 4.3 percent in vocational courses, and 10.9 percent in other courses in 1974–75. Even so, between 1964–65 and 1974–75 the number of registered Indian students rose from 53,464 to 86,144, and the participation rate for these young people aged 4–18 rose from 74 percent in 1969–70 to 83 percent in 1974–75.

Although there are undoubtedly some differences in emphasis in the education systems of Canada and the United States, there are probably more similarities. There are special problems with inner-city schools. There are problems of relating properly to linguistic and ethnic minority groups. It is perhaps apparent in both countries that a more sophisticated and individualized approach is required if the educational and personal needs of all students are to be adequately met.

The last few years have seen the discovery in North America of a whole group of social services not previously perceived as having much in common or even being particularly important. Frequently these services have simply been called "social," but it is often useful, especially for purposes of international communication and comparison, to call education, health, income-maintenance, housing, and employment services "social services." Kamerman and Kahn, United States scholars in social policy analysis and development, have suggested, as the British Fabian Society has, that the personal social services in fact constitute a "sixth" social service.

So far as the personal social services are concerned, the Canada Assistance Plan has led to a grouping or regrouping of services usually under the provincial departments of social services. While not exactly like the British model of free-standing social service departments, there are many similarities. This model has proved attractive in both Canada and the United States. Separation of income assistance and personal social service programs in the United States, imitated to some extent in Canada, has made it more possible to see the personal social services as a distinct sector. There has in both countries been a substantial growth in public expenditures on the personal social services since the early 1960s. In fact, so much was this the case that by the early 1970s the official view in the United States was that these expenditures were "uncontrollable." As a consequence, in October, 1972, the United States Congress placed a ceiling on the total amount of expenditures to be shared with the states to assist supporting many social programs. In the United States the 1974 social services amendments and Title XX of the Social Security Act sought to bring greater order and equity by requiring all states to engage in a public planning process for the personal social services, and on the basis of such planning to submit claims for revenue sharing to the federal government. Title XX was intended, therefore, to regulate expenditures, to insure equity between states, and to provide an ongoing, though limited, commitment to support of the personal social services.

The personal social services in Canada in both the public and private sectors have grown significantly in the last fifteen years. Their funding base is still linked in the main, however, to the financial mechanism for providing income assistance to poor people. There are insufficient funds available in the nongovernment sector to provide a wholly viable voluntary system of services. What perhaps remains in doubt in both the United States and Canada is whether the growth of the recent past has been sufficient to move the personal social services from a residual to a more respected and institutionalized role in the two countries.

Public housing accommodates perhaps 2 percent of households in Canada, and of these more than half involve old people and the remainder, low-income families. The proportions in the United States are roughly similar. Public housing units represented about 1.6 percent of all housing units in 1976. About one quarter of these units were designed for persons sixty-two years old or over and disabled or handicapped people.

Housing, then, in North America may be seen as a social policy issue rather than a social service matter. There has been concern about living conditions, especially in cities, for at least a century. The solution sought lay primarily in the public regulation of private construction. It was not until the 1930s in both the United States and Canada that federal legislation provided for any more direct involvement in the housing field. The goal embodied in succeeding pieces of American legislation has remained "that every American family have a decent home and a suitable living environment." That goal has yet to be achieved.

The income-security programs of the United States and Canada are largely the product of the last four or five decades. These programs have grown dramatically, and all are undergoing constant review and monitoring. How to maintain current benefit levels for ever-expanding population groups such as the aged while at the same time curtailing costs is an ever-challenging issue. So also is the issue of universality versus means testing.

The provision of medical care is another issue of concern, though more so in the United States than in Canada. In Canada there is a national medical care insurance scheme, intended to provide access to medical care for all Canadians. The United States does not as yet have such a system, even though it is one of the highest spenders on health care in the world.

EUROPE

Both unemployment (especially among the more vulnerable groups) and inflation are rising.

Most of the countries have been confronted with the necessity of cutting public social budgets (including social security).

The public expenditures in Sweden and the Netherlands, respectively 67 percent and 60 percent of the net national income, are the highest in the world. In the Netherlands, for example, the social welfare expenditures of the national ministries charged with education, labor and social affairs, health, and social and cultural services increased in the last five years from 25 billion florins to 50 billion florins—about 50 percent of the total public budget. Social security benefits increased from 3.5 billion florins in 1960 to 72.6 billion in 1980! Approximately 65 percent of the social security benefits are received by the so-called "nonactive" people: unemployed, sick, handicapped, aged, or beneficiaries of the Social Assistance Act. One can discover similar developments in other Western European countries.

Most of the reports explain the difficult ways and methods in which efforts are undertaken to cut private wages and the public budgets, including social security subsystems, without affecting in a socially unacceptable way the most vulnerable groups. The United Kingdom report mentions three main trends in this respect in that country:

1. There has been a complete review of the social security system, with fairly substantial changes in the administration of supplementary benefits (social assistance). There have already

been two major reports and a White Paper announcing government intentions.

2. As a result of a Royal Commission, the government has decided to alter the general administration of the health service, and legislation to do this will be before Parliament during the present session. It is not likely to alter the service, but its administration will be somewhat changed.

3. Finally, the personal social services of local authorities are being scrutinized, with special emphasis on expenditure levels. There is a great deal of controversy about the effectiveness of these services and how they will continue in view of the present economic crisis. This is linked with the government's announced intention of allowing more autonomy in public expenditure to local authorities.

All European countries, then, in varying degrees, are faced with major challenges in the continued provision of adequate social welfare services and in the proper role of government. Addressing these issues in a decade of low if not zero economic growth will be no easy task.

THE FUTURE OF SOCIAL WELFARE

What seem to be the prospects for the future social development programs, given the present and likely long-time period of economic uncertainty as reported by the regional reports from around the world? For the greater part of the world's population, the prospect seems bleak; for others, there is a possibility of slighter lower standards of living; and for relatively few, little more than inconvenience.

The report from Asia indicates that in 1980 the outlook is pessimistic: economic understanding of social welfare programs is usually based on Western models which are often not appropriate to the Asian continent; rapid population increases can be expected to continue; many administrative models have become outmoded, and present planning is overcentralized and defective.

The report from the OECD countries refers to the prospects for the 1980s as "very somber." Among the most difficult challenges facing these nations during the period of projected negative economic growth is how to share rights and opportunities fairly. The ideal of equality and the concept of equity are seriously hampered during restrictive economic periods; public social budgets are reduced, and a severe reordering of priorities can bring about societal upheaval.

In Latin America, the ups and downs in the international monetary markets; the growth in real terms of energy cost; the protectionist policies developed to defend employment levels in those countries; and the prospects of a decade which begins with trends toward recession and rising inflation without any prospect of a sounder, more stable, international order that reflects quantum leaps toward equity in the distribution of the world's resources do not augur an optimistic picture for social and economic well-being for the years to come. Small economies in Latin America which base their development strategies on entering the international market will undoubtedly be adversely affected in the event this scenario is confirmed. The flow of foreign currencies to foreign export sales is the cornerstone for strengthening the capacity for investment and growth, and the implementation of any employment policy may be affected and have an adverse impact on foreign accounts. The realities of staggering export-import imbalance, reduction in the growth of productivity, rising unemployment and underemployment, and the slowdown in income and income distribution will have a drastic and negative impact on the economic and social conditions of people in the region. On the other hand, measures that may be taken in several areas toward establishing an international order, characterized by a more equitable relationship will have a direct influence on efforts aimed at social progress.

The guarantee of a minimum standard of living to all citizens is one of the main achievements of modern welfare states. In periods of economic uncertainty it is tempting to tinker with existing social provisions on the grounds that programs can be made more effective and dollars spent more wisely. Some social provisions are more susceptible to this tinkering than are others, and more so than programs for the poor. Recent attempts in the North American Region (Canada and the United States), to reform the income-maintenance system have been frustrated by the work ethic and the mentality of the English Poor Law, both ingrained in the cultural fabric of both countries. The relevance of these socioeconomic barriers to the structurally unemployed and, indeed, to the economy as a whole is not completely obvious when there are too few jobs for those in the labor market. The drastic cutbacks in social programs that are occurring have not yet had their full impact on the people of these countries. It is apparent, however, that life is becoming more and more difficult for those who are the victims of inflation, unemployment, and the absence of personal social services.

How then to proceed? What priorities for social development should be adopted? Demographic changes make adjustments in some social provisions desirable. There is sufficient knowledge about these changes to be able to plan realistically at national and local levels, and to remedy the major deficiencies in social programs. The North American Region reports the need to reinforce universalist principles wherever feasible. It should seek to balance the interests of children, of the elderly and the handicapped, of recently admitted refugees, of families, and of the work force. It should seek to respond to major social changes promptly and effectively. In periods of social and economic uncertainty policies must be adopted that promote social cohesion and that reduce social divisions in the respective countries.

The prospect for social welfare in Australia, as observed by Edna R. Chamberlain, seems to have universal applicability when considering the future role of social welfare in social development in a period of economic uncertainty:

> The proliferation of varieties of human service personnel is chaotic and confusing. Social workers have to date failed to identify the essential service functions that underlie the labels and the objectives these functions are intended to achieve. Also, they have failed to define their own functions. If social workers are to be distinguished from other workers in the welfare field, it must be by something more than time spent in an educational institution.

A major difference in social provision by the end of the next decade will, I believe, be a much higher degree of integration in the human services. The lack of coordination of programs, particularly between health and welfare, has been a worrying feature of recent years, but the move toward integration would seem to be strengthening at the top policy-planning level, and on the ground. . . .

In the final analysis, attitude is as important as resources. In most countries there is still no clear ideological commitment on the political level to major social services as a major component of social development. Indeed, one of the peculiarities of the social services is that though they are most often provided publicly and most often on the universal position, they are received and enjoyed privately. It has been suggested that they are public cures for private ills; they are a response to social conditions but only seldom provide the basis for social action for social and economic change. Even in the best of times, without a strong and vocal constituency for social welfare, a comprehensive, universally available system, economic uncertainty simply provides an easy excuse for delaying reforms.

The development of social programs has been piecemeal and incremental; in developed and developing countries alike, there has not been a comprehensive design or ideological commitment that has support across all groups in the society. The dismantling of these programs, therefore, if that has to happen, will more than likely be similarly fragmented. The best hope is in the political will that develops along with the programs themselves, and with their universal popularity.

The past fifty years represent what in historical perspective can only be called a record of unprecedented economic and social progress. And while the distribution of the benefits of this phenomenon have clearly not been evenly distributed, they have helped allocate prosperity at least somewhat more equally. A great deal more needs to be done. While in earlier times the resources were more abundant than the political will, the future is likely to see a reversal of that premise. The one overriding fact that emerges is that there is no turning back. There are still huge maldistributions in wealth and income. There are differences in well-being between geographic regions of the world and within countries in each region of the world, between the employed and unemployed, the able-bodied and the handicapped, the sexes, the ethnic groups, and so on. But the differences are in most cases smaller than before. With renewed commitment for changes that address the "have-nots" of the world, and new roles for the ICSW in using its network for change, the well-being of people throughout the world can and must be achieved.

THE REFUGEE CHALLENGE: THE CURRENT PRIORITY

Probably no single human tragedy commands the attention of persons concerned with social and economic policies for human well-being more than that of the world's refugees—the world's have-nots. To be sure, the refugee problem is replete with political issues within the countries of origin of refugees and among countries of asylum for, or sought as countries of asylum by, the refugees. Political, technical, ideological, and legal issues notwithstanding, it seems to this ICSW world rapporteur that more than passing reference must be given at the XXth International Conference on Social Welfare to a matter of international dimensions that affects the basic human rights of millions of men, women, and children. These are people forced to leave their homes and lands for many reasons, for as many reasons as one may assign to violence, conflict, and oppression within and among nations of the world.

The definition of the term "refugee" used by most governments and international organizations was stated some thirty years ago by the United Nations Convention on the Status of Refugees and applied by the United Nations High Commissioner for Refugees:

Any person who . . . owing to well-founded fear of being persecuted for reasons of race, religion, nationality, membership in a particular social group or political opinion, is outside the country of his nationality and is unable or, owing to such fear, is unwilling to avail himself of the protection of that country; or who, not having a nationality and being outside the country of his former habitual residence as a result of such events, is unable or owing to such fear, is unwilling to return to it.

The principal phrases of that definition are that the person is outside his or her country of origin because of his or her "well-founded" fear of persecution upon return. These refugees are men, women, and children who are in what seems like unending transit, who are homeless, or who are "strangers" in the countries of asylum and among people many of whom reject them or, at best, are ambivalent about their presence because of economic and social conditions within their country.

Only the North American regional report gave attention to the increasing seriousness of this human problem. The report of the United States ICSW committee referring to the refugee problem stated:

It constitutes only a variant of a large, worldwide problem, namely, the absorption of poverty-stricken populations in developing countries of the world by countries which are developed and therefore more capable of "sharing their wealth" . . . . It reflects an international phenomenon, namely, the unequal distribution of wealth and population in the world, and the fact that overpopulation and hunger require international arrangements including redistribution of resources on an international scale.

Statistics on refugees, a population so large and fluid, defy absolute accuracy. The year 1964 was the first one in which the United States Committee for Refugees published what is now an annual survey. In 1964 the total number of refugees was just under 8 million. Year by year, the number has increased as the war escalated in Vietnam, as strife swept parts of Asia, Africa, and Latin America. By 1967, the total had doubled to 16 million and reached its peak of 17.5 million in 1970. The 1980s already give evidence of further increases: refugees fleeing Afghanistan into Pakistan; a flow of people from the Ethiopian desert into Somalia; close to 75,000 people leaving Cuba for the United States within one three-week period.

Hard Times and the Search for a Frugal Utopia

JOHN F. JONES
CHAIRMAN, BOARD OF STUDIES IN SOCIAL WORK, CHINESE UNIVERSITY OF HONG KONG

Current trends point to a somber future for the world economy and international relations. A painful outlook for the poorer countries with no end to poverty and hunger; continuing world stagnation combined with inflation; international monetary disorder; mounting debts and deficits; protectionism; major tensions between countries competing for energy, food, and raw materials; growing world population and more unemployment in North and South; increasing threats to the environment and the international commons through deforestation and desertification, overfishing and overgrazing, the pollution of air and water. And overshadowing everything the arms race.[1]

THESE WORDS of the Brandt Commission reflect what is gradually becoming a consensus of opinion as we enter the last decades of the twentieth century, haunted by the tensions of global politics and the state of the world economy. Adding to the alarm is the realization of the potentially explosive disparity in development between the Northern Hemisphere and the Southern Hemisphere. The geography is imprecise, but the North-South division illustrates the position of the industrially prosperous nations concentrated in the Northern Hemisphere who, even when deprived of natural materials, still outstrip those largely Southern Hemisphere countries which remain impoverished despite rich resources. At present three quarters of mankind exist on roughly one fifth of the world's resources. About 800 million live in desperate poverty. The average person in the industrialized North can expect to live to seventy, has at least a primary education, and does not go

---

[1] *North-South: a Program for Survival,* **Report of the Independent Commission on International Development Issues under the chairmanship of Willy Brandt (London: Pan Books, 1980), p. 46.**

hungry. Life expectancy among the great majority of people in the South is closer to fifty; in the poorest countries one out of four children dies before the age of five; one fifth or more of the South's population suffer from malnutrition; and half are illiterate.

Nor does the future suggest a reversal of current trends. There is ample reason to suppose that the combined debt of the Third World, which has grown from $70 billion in 1970 to $300 billion a decade later, will keep on increasing. For the rich industrial nations of the North the quintupling of oil prices in the mid-1970s and the doubling in the past year has been a major cause of inflation. For the South it has been disastrous. A mounting financial deficit has helped to arrest development in some countries and led to talk of national bankruptcy in others. The manufactured goods which the South buys from the North have become relatively more expensive than most of the raw materials the developing countries sell. Also, the aid programs of the North have been cut in an attempt to combat public spending and inflation. In only one area does public spending continue to grow out of all proportion: national defense. Military spending, now well exceeding $400 billion annually, eats up resources and energies which could be devoted to world development.

The state of what the United Nations euphemistically calls "the least developed countries" is especially distressing. These are countries with severe long-term constraints on development assessed on three basic criteria: per capita gross national product (GNP) of $100 or less at 1970 prices, share of manufacturing of 10 percent or less of gross domestic product (GDP), and 20 percent or less of literate persons aged fifteen or more. The least developed countries have a total population of approximately 260 million. Their average per capita income in 1977 was about $150 (equivalent to $80 in 1970 prices), with an annual per capita growth rate of less than one percent. The condition of the poorer countries worsened in the 1970s in important sectors such as agriculture.[2] Agricul-

[2] Department of International Economic and Social Affairs, *World Economic Survey, 1977* (New York: United Nations, 1978), pp. 4–5.

ture provides 44 percent of the least developed countries' GDP and over 83 percent of their employment. These countries do not grow enough to feed themselves, and there are indications that in ten years' time they may face shortages amounting to a third of their present consumption.

It should be remembered that most of the world's poverty is rural. The urban poverty of Calcutta or Rio de Janeiro is dramatic and apparent, but for all its drama, it is probably less terrible and certainly less pervasive than the rural poverty of Bangladesh or Chad. A good 70 percent of the poor in Asia or Africa live in the countryside, a fact often overlooked in national planning for such social services as health care, education, housing, or indeed the most basic items like water. The injustice of rural poverty is aggravated by the inequities of land ownership. In many countries a minority of landlords and large farmers, perhaps as few as 5 percent or 10 percent of rural households, own as much as 60 percent of arable land.

The total financing needs of the least developed countries are estimated to be around $11 billion per annum for the coming decade and $21 billion per annum for the 1990s, based on the target of an annual GDP growth rate of 6.5 percent, and a rate of growth of domestic savings of 6.8 percent. The developing world has had to borrow in order to finance its social and economic progress and sometimes simply to survive. The massive indebtedness of developing countries could lead to disaster.

The key factor behind this grim outlook is the world's energy situation. With a tight, long-term oil supply situation, oil prices are likely to continue rising in real terms. This will bring about a shift in the terms of trade in favor of OPEC over the the next decade, but this will not necessarily benefit other Third World countries. The oil-importing developing countries obtain about two thirds of their commercial energy from oil. Although most countries of the South consume only a modest amount of oil, they must expand their use of oil and other commercial forms of energy as they industrialize. While consumption of commercial energy doubled in the North between 1960 and 1976, it tripled in the South, although it was still just one fifteenth of the West's consumption or one twelfth of Eastern Europe's. Even now, the developing countries import only about one tenth of all traded oil. For everyone the sharp rise in oil prices has become a major cause of stagflation, but the ones that suffer most are low-income countries.

Recently, banks have begun to sound ominous warnings that the balance-of-payments deficits of many non-oil-producing Third World countries are reaching the unmanageable stage and certainly are beyond the ability of commercial banks to finance. Some European leaders have implied that it is also beyond the scope of the West's aid programs to rectify the situation. As Britain's Prime Minister Margaret Thatcher pointed out in the recent Venice summit, all the official aid given by the Western countries to the developing nations as a whole has not been sufficient to match the increase they have had to bear in the price of oil since 1978. Because of the immense rise in oil prices since the beginning of 1979, the Organization of Petroleum Exporting Countries (OPEC) nations will have surplus revenues around $131 billion in 1980.

During the 1973–74 oil price increase, commercial banks were expected to shoulder responsibility for recycling the petrodollars by lending to developing countries. But the process cannot be attempted again since it is now altogether harder to find credit-worthy borrowers. In 1974–78, non-oil-producing nations more than doubled their foreign debt, from $142 billion to $315 billion. Commercial banks provided more than 60 percent of the loans. Central banks are now worried about the possibility of a massive debt default, with a financial panic leading to a worldwide depression.[3]

THE WORLD ECONOMY'S SOCIAL CONSEQUENCES

The social dimensions of the economic crisis are not hard to imagine, and the consequences of a recession for health, hous-

[3] Ho Kwon Ping, "Alarm Bells Are Ringing over the Massive Debt Crisis," *Far Eastern Economic Review* (May 2, 1980), 108(19):41.

ing, and education are too serious not to be noted in passing.

Ill health continues to afflict the Third World, which is in no way surprising considering the poverty, malnutrition, poor hygiene, and inadequate sanitation. Roughly one billion people are at risk from malaria. Blindness afflicts 30 to 40 million people in developing countries. Infant and child mortality is high. There are African countries where one child in four dies before the first birthday. Sleeping sickness afflicts 35 million people. Bilharzia claims perhaps as many as 200 million victims. Even seen from a purely economic viewpoint where people are just human resources, a poverty-stricken population suffering from malnutrition and parasitic diseases cannot fully farm rich agricultural lands, and must lower productivity. Taking another point of view, it is salutary to remember that the world's military expenditures in only half a day would be sufficient to finance the entire malaria eradication program of the World Health Organization. That is another story touching on the bad economics of warfare.

The problems of housing are very easy to understand in Hong Kong, which has experienced a tenfold population increase over the past thirty years. Looking at the world's population, we know that conservative projections for the next thirty years envisage a doubling of the world's present 4.3 billion population. That calls for duplicating every building, service, and place of employment if existing standards are to be maintained. Obviously, present standards are far from ideal. Towns and cities throughout the world are beset by problems of unemployment, underemployment, pollution, crowding, squatter settlements, slums, inadequate public transportation, social alienation, and crime. Many urban areas lack such essentials as sanitation, electricity, and water. In poorer countries housing conditions are deplorable.

Basic education as well as technological training necessary for agricultural and industrial progress remains a worldwide problem. The simplest yardstick, literacy, reveals the urgency of the situation even where it shows modest advances. In developing countries about one third of adults were literate in 1950: in 1970 just over one half were. In Latin America literacy rose from 65 percent in 1960 to 75 percent in 1970; in

Asia, from 45 percent to 75 percent over the same period; and in Africa, from 20 percent to 26 percent. There are still some thirty-four countries where over 80 percent of the population cannot read or write. Under these conditions, economic and social development are difficult.

What makes the social situation so disheartening is that improvement would seem to demand an expanding economy at the very time a recession or worse is in sight. The Western industrial economy, which grew at a rate of 4.0 percent or 5.0 percent from 1950 to 1973, slowed to an average rate of 2.5 percent annual increase between 1973 and 1979. The East European economies also experienced a slowing down in the past few years, although figures are not always comparable. In the least developed countries, exports have stagnated. The countries of the South need money, and that is slow in coming. While most industrialized countries have accepted the target of 0.7 percent of GNP for official aid, they have fallen down on their commitment.

ASIA

In Asia, where national plans call for growth, the oil shock has already had a depressive effect on developing economies without at the same time being deflationary. The influence of increased oil, fertilizer, and petrochemical prices with their effects on the cost of production in agriculture, mining, manufacturing, power, and transportation is likely to spur inflation to greater heights. The depressive effects of a cost-price squeeze, which developing countries already feel when trying to sell their exports, will be reinforced if a worldwide recession occurs. Then perhaps prices will stabilize, but only after there are decreased levels of production in the industrial and commercial sectors. The extent to which agriculture suffers will vary with dependence on export markets and on the ability of governments to sustain a market for domestically consumed agricultural products.[4]

Asia is very vulnerable to a recession. Four of its large coun-

---

[4] Economic and Social Commission for Asia and the Pacific, *Economic and Social Survey of Asia and the Pacific, 1979: Recent Economic Development, 1978–1979* (Bangkok: United Nations, 1980), pp. 122–24.

tries—India, Bangladesh, Pakistan, and Indonesia—contain about two thirds of the world's poor. The Asian poverty belt has experienced a rapid population growth which the cultivable land cannot easily accommodate. In Bangladesh, for instance, about one third of the people are marginal peasants with less than one hectare of land, poor tenant farmers, or sharecroppers. Another third are landless peasants. Even if land reform were pushed, its benefits would be small since large holdings account for only 0.2 percent of the total land. Extensive (and expensive) irrigation projects would be required to increase yield. The need for water conservancy and irrigation holds true in most of Asia. Stating the priority of agriculture does not imply that industry is unimportant in the region. India, Pakistan, and Indonesia are major producers of manufactures, and Indonesia produces oil. But these countries remain predominantly agricultural; for the countryside is where the mass of the people live, and each country depends heavily on the export of raw materials. In this they are typical of the Third World: rich in natural resources, lacking equitable trade arrangements, and strapped for money.

An important institution for economic development in the region is the Asian Development Bank (ADB). Bank lending during 1979 reached $1,252 million compared to $660 million in 1975. One third of the bank's loan commitments in 1979 were made on concessional terms to the poorer countries in the region. These soft loans, which carry no interest and are made for long periods, are crucial to Asia's least developed countries. Most of the Asian Development Fund (ADF) loans go to countries with a per capita GNP below $200, such as Bangladesh, Burma, Laos, the Maldives, Nepal, Sri Lanka, and Vietnam. (India has not so far borrowed from this source.) But soft lending is where the ADB appears to be facing the worst problems at present. The ADF, which makes soft loans, carrying only a one percent service charge, has been temporarily closed because of replenishment difficulties.

The total $6.7 billion which the bank has committed in ordinary and soft loans during the fourteen years of its existence is very small in comparision with the total inflow of funds into

The Search for a Frugal Utopia 41

the region from bilateral and multilateral sources as well as from commercial banks. Allowing for the fact that the $6.7 billion will lead to investments totaling $16.5 billion when the contributions of borrowing countries and cofinanciers are added in, the amount is still small in relation to total resource transfers to the region. Although the ADB hopes to commit a further $3.7 billion of ordinary loan funds and $1.7 billion of soft loans by the end of 1982, this again falls far short of meeting Asia's expanding capital needs. By the end of this decade, the bank's borrowing member countries will require net external resource transfers in excess of $50 billion annually compared to just $11 billion in 1978. While large in nominal terms, these estimated capital needs represent only a modest increase in real, inflation-adjusted terms.[5]

In the Asian and Pacific region, the momentum of real growth, measured in GDP, slowed considerably in 1979. Apart from delaying the solution of the massive and urgent socio-economic problems of the area, the energy crisis coincided with a downturn in rice and cereal production, accelerating inflation, and a higher combined balance of trade deficit. For many Asian countries, the oil price hikes came at the worst possible time, hamstringing efforts to escape crippling poverty and forcing countries into deeper debt.

EMERGENCY MEASURES FOR SURVIVAL

With such problems besetting the South and in consequence the North, it is natural to hope for a master plan, preferably an international one, to save the world. Indeed, the Brandt Commission's report presents just that when recommending emergency measures for 1980–85: increased development aid, energy cooperation, food production, and economic reform.[6]

At the government level, developing nations—especially the poverty belts of Africa and Asia—need at least $4 billion of extra aid annually for the next twenty years to become self-

[5] Anthony Rowley, "The ADB's Decade of Crisis," *Far Eastern Economic Review*, (May 16, 1980), 108(21):55–58.
[6] *North-South: A Program for Survival*, pp. 276–81.

sustaining. This means doubling the present annual official development aid to reach the recognized 0.7 target of GNP by 1985. Increased lending by commercial banks on a guaranteed basis, increased official aid, expanded lending by the World Bank and the various regional development banks, the use of International Monetary Fund (IMF) gold, and other resource-transfer mechanisms could raise the flow of funds to developing regions to the sum of $50–60 billion annually within the next five years.

In exchange for stiff conservation measures and an agreement to index the price of oil to the real value of a group of strong currencies, oil-exporting countries should guarantee levels of production and avoid drastic price hikes. In addition, there should be a special multinational financing institution for investment in oil and natural gas exploration and development in the Third World.

In order to overcome food deficits in poor countries and to ease inflationary pressures in the world food market, an intensive program to increase food production in the South is necessary. Massive investment in agriculture mean that an extra $8 billion in aid must be provided annually to developing countries specifically for agricultural development. As part of a long-term strategy, multilateral agencies should provide adjustment assistance for land reform.

There should be a new international monetary system with more stable exchange rates, shared responsibility between surplus and deficit countries for adjusting balance-of-payments disequilibria, and an orderly expansion of world liquidity. This would imply liberalizing the international trading system and allowing developing countries in the process of industrialization to expand their markets. The IMF, too, should adopt a more flexible attitude toward the balance-of-payments adjustment problems of developing nations. It should therefore not insist on severe deflationary measures as standard policy, but should consider more sympathetically the socioeconomic objectives of the Third World.

The Brandt Commission has been criticized for, among other things, its limited attention to the role of the private sector. The commission members looked to government rather than to the individual to solve problems, it is alleged, thus favoring central bureaucracies over the entrepreneur. The comment is not without merit, especially when the need for individual incentives has become apparent even in command economies such as China's. But perhaps a more serious weakness of the Brandt blueprint lies in its genesis as a commission report, lacking substantial support (other than lip service) from governments and dependent upon the least reliable of factors—international accord. While this criticism may seem fainthearted and appear to downplay the necessity of international cooperation (an interpretation I would regret), it is still true that global plans have their shortcomings. More realistic models for progress, perhaps, can be found in the workaday programs of governments for regional and national development since they tend to be more pragmatic, more subject to accountability, and slightly more predictable regarding outcome. Such plans are maybe less systematic because of compromise and more inconsistent than ideal development would be, but trial and error have concrete lessons to teach.

NATIONAL DEVELOPMENT MODELS

When looking for development models, Asia again comes to mind if only because, side by side with underdevelopment, the most dynamic economies in the world today are in Asia—Japan, Hong Kong, South Korea, Singapore, and Taiwan. The common method of growth—an economy based on industries and services and less on agriculture—might also seem to point the way for developing countries since productivity based on agriculture has inherent limits whereas an industrial-based economy has a tendency to expand.[7] (It should be noted, however, that two of these countries, South Korea and Taiwan, carried out extensive land reform as a prelude to, and prerequisite of, development.) The economies of this "Gang of Five" have experienced high growth rates in real output with the performance of other indicators, such as capital investment and productivity, equally impressive.

Take Taiwan, for instance. Taiwan's exports in 1979 ex-

[7] See Edward K. Y. Chen, *Hyper-growth in Asian Economies: A Comparative Study of Hong Kong, Japan, Korea, Singapore and Taiwan* (London: Macmillan, 1979).

ceeded $16 billion—up 27 percent from the previous year. Foreign investments increased by 54 percent, amounting to $328 million. As elsewhere, economic growth slowed down and there was inflation, but the economy still grew by 8 percent and the inflation rate is expected not to pass 10 percent in 1980. As the result of a labor squeeze, wages are, next to Japan's, the highest in Asia. Individual income exceeded $1,700 in 1979 and will probably top the $2,000 mark in 1980. Speaking in a very general fashion, affluence, if not shared evenly, is at least distributed widely, judged by the "comfort index" of television sets, motor scooters, recreation facilities, and other consumer commodities and services.

To make the case for *laissez-faire* economies based on the hypergrowth states of Taiwan, Hong Kong, Japan, South Korea, and Singapore would be to oversimplify the Asia capitalist model. Apart from Hong Kong—and even here the government has sided actively with big business—none of these countries has given the market forces free rein. These governments have intervened ubiquitously in the economy, and the architects of economic policy preside at the ministerial level. Japan's number one assumption that the business of government is business is well known. The Taipei government engineered a very successful land reform program and subsequent industrialization, pioneering along the way the concept of export-processing zones. The Singapore government conglomerate is an extensive one, engaging in all major enterprises. It has not hesitated to impose wage restraints or to control the availability of workers. It would seem that, in the opinion of Asia's best and brightest policy-makers, the effectiveness of the free market is an illusion.

The affluence, where once there was poverty, of Asia's dynamic economies gives their development strategies some credibility in the eyes of poorer neighbors. Nothing succeeds like success. Yet a serious objection to taking these hypergrowth states as models is that they are relatively wealthy industrialized countries, and we are looking for a model that more truly represents the majority of the world's population. Here in Hong Kong we do not have to look far for a very instructive illustration of development: the People's Republic of China.

THE CHINA SYNDROME

I suggest China as a development model hesitantly and with no sense of euphoria. I am aware of its serious failures in human rights, most notably during the Cultural Revolution, and of its political expediency when supporting, for instance, the barbarous Pol Pot regime in Kampuchea. Moreover, from a narrow economic viewpoint, some of China's current development programs rest on assumptions still to be tested, and there is a strong element of wishful thinking in its modernization plans. The single most important determinant of China's economic future into the 1990s will be its ability to increase agricultural production by more than 2 percent annually to keep ahead of population growth.[8] Another hesitation in making China the exemplar of development arises from the inconsistency of its industrial policy in the past. Should the present leadership falter and the radicals once more come to power, who knows how the model might be altered?

With these reservations, a strong argument still remains for seeing in China a model for developing countries. China undoubtedly belongs to the Third World. Although its GNP probably falls within the world's top ten countries, its per capita income puts China somewhere between 90th and 100th place. Furthermore, it is primarily an agricultural country, with that sector engaging some 80 percent of the population directly. Besides that, agriculture supplies the materials for another 10 percent of the population working in light industry, and it provides capital accumulation for heavy industry.

The chronology of China's modern development begins with the Communist liberation in 1949. Since then China has succeeded, by and large, in abolishing starvation and abject poverty. With only 7 percent of the world's arable land, China feeds a fifth of the world's population. Production has gener-

[8] Allen S. Whiting and Robert F. Dernberger, *China's Future: Foreign Policy and Economic Development in the Post-Mao Era* (New York: McGraw-Hill, 1977), pp. 125–40.

ally kept up with population growth, and grain output which in 1957 was put at 175 million tons reached 304 million tons in 1978. The fact that China imports 6 to 10 million tons of grain annually, some have argued, is due to inadequate transportation more than to a shortfall in production.[9] The country's industrial output increased between 1949 and the mid-1970s at an average rate of approximately 13 percent, or a doubling of the level of output every five years. It is true that wages are low and vary somewhat according to geographical location, type of employment, and the rural/urban differential. Nonetheless, the average Chinese now enjoys a stable livelihood, and there is a wide dissemination of benefits accruing from health, education, and welfare programs.

To comment in detail on China's progress over the last three decades is impossible, but one can isolate some dilemmas which China, along with other developing nations, has had to face. Four such development dilemmas in particular seem relevant not only to China but to the Third World as a whole: the agriculture vs. industry dilemma, the independence vs. dependence dilemma, the participation vs. mobilization dilemma, and the now vs. the future dilemma.[10]

Agriculture vs. industry. Nations which have concentrated on urban industrialization while ignoring the needs of the majority of the people living in the countryside have usually exploited the rural population by taking much and giving little. It is ironic that in many parts of the world those engaged in agriculture and feeding others themselves enjoy the lowest nutrition levels. At the same time, industrial advancement is an absolute necessity for the Third World and demands heavy investment. What can be done? It is in this context that China's stress on agriculture since the late 1950s and the Maoist formulation, "to walk on two legs" (that is, not to rely exclusively on industrialization), makes sense. China's first Five-Year Plan, 1953–57, was heavily influenced by models in-

---

[9] Michael Yahuda, "China," in *Asia and Pacific Review* (Saffron Walden: World of Information, 1980), p. 195.

[10] These are dealt with more fully but less schematically in John F. Jones, ed., *Building China: Studies in Integrated Development* (Hong Kong: Chinese University Press, 1980), a collection of essays on the Chinese experience by various scholars.

spired by the Soviet Union. The plan placed most emphasis on achieving early industrialization and, virtually ignoring agriculture, sought to concentrate state resources on the rapid development of heavy industry. Giant factories, mines, and engineering projects, almost all located in or near large cities, were given priority. Fifty-eight percent of the 42 billion *yuen* allocated for the plan was to go to industry while only 7.6 percent was allocated to agriculture. But as early as 1956 Chinese leaders expressed doubts about the utility of the Soviet model. Giving priority to heavy industry while ignoring small-scale production and agriculture had jeopardized long-term industrialization. They came to see that only a more productive and efficient agricultural establishment could finance industrialization. By 1957, gains in agriculture were declining, a development that had to be changed. Mao's answer was a radical organizational one—the creation of the People's Communes—as well as a compromise policy statement: "Let agriculture be the foundation, and industry the leading factor." Neither the communes, which were meant to integrate the functions of government, agriculture, industry, commerce, and social welfare, nor the sudden shift in economic priorities symbolized by the Great Leap Forward, were instant successes. Nevertheless, over the long haul, much of the old imbalance between industry and agriculture was corrected. The grain output, for example, grew at the unusually rapid rate of almost 6 percent annually between 1964 and 1967. This was probably due to the manufacture of producer goods for agriculture, such as agricultural machinery and chemical fertilizer, the extension of water management and irrigation, and the introduction of new rice varieties. But the diminishing returns of these innovations accounted for a drop in production subsequently. The country is not yet out of the woods in respect to agriculture. Agricultural development will continue to put a severe constraint on overall economic and social progress unless productivity surpasses an annual growth rate of 2 percent over the next ten or fifteen years. That is why the Chinese leadership has selected agriculture as one of the four areas for modernization.

Independence vs. dependence. The alarming indebtedness of

the Third World would seem to establish a case for self-sufficiency and the avoidance of credit. But development can hardly occur without borrowing; even deficits, kept within bounds, have their purpose. China has wobbled in its national and international banking policy, never quite sure how much it could safely borrow. The Chinese have tended to favor a conservative approach to credit. In the 1950s China had a deficit in trade for five years; since that time there have been only six overall deficits, each springing from exceptional or unusual circumstances.[11] Yet, as regards trade, the Chinese have perhaps been more steadfast to self-sufficiency in doctrine than in practice. Only during the Cultural Revolution (1966–69) did the Chinese pursue a strict policy of self-dependence, with a resulting decline in imports of producer goods. During the 1970s, the growth in imports of producer goods and the signing of contracts for the delivery of complete plants showed a willingness to rely on imports of producer goods and foreign technology to achieve domestic industrialization.[12] With a two-way foreign trade now approaching $30 billion China cannot afford to turn down the offers of big loans from foreign banks, and financiers believe that the Chinese will increasingly act on existing options in order to finance the modernization program. Foreign investment is likely to assume greater and greater importance in the years ahead not only in boosting export earnings by refurbishing the country's light industries, but also in huge projects such as prospecting and drilling for oil in the South China Sea. China is now a member of both the IMF and the World Bank, giving it access to concessional loans. But it is in its commercial banking system that the most revolutionary changes are occurring, and that appears to be on the verge of becoming a most profitable enterprise.[13]

---

[11] Christopher Howe, *China's Economy: A Basic Guide* (London: Paul Elek, 1978), pp. 148–49.

[12] Whiting and Dernberger, *China's Future,* pp. 170–72.

[13] See "Focus: Banking '80," *Far Eastern Economic Review* (April 4, 1980), 108(14):37–104, and esp. David Bonavia, "No Big Loans Yet but Soon China Must Act on Options," p. 85.

Participation vs. mobilization. China's programs and projects—water conservancy, education, agriculture, health care, and industrial enterprises—suggest an organization-intensive system. The question arises: how far is the organization voluntary and how far coercive? Clearly there are ideological constraints which do not tolerate deviation. The harsh treatment of Peking's Democratic Wall movement of 1978–79 and the suppression of the young dissidents are reminders of that. However, within the limits imposed by the political structure and philosophy, tolerance for individual initiative and disagreement has varied considerably. Taken as a whole, China can be said to have a "command economy," but the phrase needs qualifying. The leadership has consistently relied on the masses for participation, consultation, support, and—to some extent—direction. Undoubtedly the economy is a planned one; yet there have been times, notably during the Great Leap Forward and the Cultural Revolution, when central planning suffered, and the disorder of the second period in particular led to local defiance of authority from 1966 to 1969. There is a lesson here: decentralization is not the opposite of coercive mobilization; decentralization can in fact be autocratic and cruel. Official interpretations of Communist China's most decentralized period, the Cultural Revolution, have changed since 1976. Initially seen as an immensely successful operation by the party to rid itself of "capitalist roaders," the movement is now seen as a "severe reversal" of the socialist revolution. Lin Piao and the Gang of Four, it is said, took advantage of errors made in the party during this time to

undermine the foundation of our socialist system, subvert the dictatorship of the proletariat, destroy the leadership of the Party, adulterate Marxism-Leninism-Mao Zedong Thought, and plunge China once again into the division and chaos abhorred by the people, into blood-baths and terror.[14]

China has begun to move more toward the middle of the road in respect to individual autonomy. The coercive elements

---

[14] Yeh Chien-ying's speech to the Fourth Plenum of the Eleventh Central Committee of the Chinese Communist Party, *Beijing Review*, October 5, 1979, p. 15.

of the commune system still exist alongside its cooperative and voluntary spirit. The state continues to control the economy. Yet in the countryside private plots and material incentives are once more favored. The urban collectives (analogous to the rural communes) have brought a large, growing sector of the economy out from under the control of the state plan. This might suggest a future mixed state-private or state-collective industrial economy.

Now vs. the future. Development programs too often are sold through a pay-now-play-later plan. The catch is that payment may be very heavy and the rewards rescheduled indefinitely. In reality, the technique works only for a time, and exhortations to sacrifice must either be replaced by genuine rewards or be backed up with force. There are three pressures moving China toward a mild consumerism, the most immediate kind of reward. One is the very success of the Communist revolution. Having achieved the abolition of grinding poverty in such a short time (a remarkable achievement for a country of 900 million), the people are experiencing rising expectations along with dissatisfaction with excessive frugality. Second, the pragmatism of the present leadership has fostered a desire, in the words of Premier Hua Kuo-feng, "to readjust, restructure, consolidate, and improve the economy." The litany of where the economy has gone wrong in the past includes the following, according to the Chinese: agricultural growth has been lopsided with too much emphasis on grain production, causing shortages of nonstaple foodstuffs; energy developments have not kept pace with the rapid industrial growth, and energy usage is not as efficient as in other countries; in the steel industry, production of ore has not matched smelting capacity, and many steel products are of inferior grade; machine manufacture is inefficient because of obsolete equipment, insufficient automation, and machine tools that are inadequate for precision production; too much capital construction is poorly planned and too much is invested in constructing production-oriented facilities at the cost of housing, education, health care, and community services; too little of the national income has gone back into consumption, with the result that incomes have shown very little increase, and little improvement has been made in the livelihood of the individual.[15] It can be seen that the modernization of the economy is linked to an effort to raise the standard of living and provide both urban and rural workers with higher incomes.

Lastly, a radical socialism which called for unlimited sacrifice and put doctrinal purity above all else, including material incentives, became meaningless to the Chinese masses in the absence of substantial improvement in the living standard. The chaos and injustice of the Cultural Revolution further disillusioned many Chinese who came to question the wisdom of jettisoning economic prosperity in the name of an ideology. Constant drudgery with little improvement to look forward to could only cast doubt upon the superiority of the socialist system among the Chinese and indeed among Third World countries. To the Third World, the success of the higher-growth Asian states (Japan, South Korea, Taiwan, Singapore, and Hong Kong) might well seem more attractive than the radical Maoist road to socialism. In part the Four Modernizations—in agriculture, industry, national defense, and science—are an admission that radical Maoism (now in disfavor) is, in the opinion of the current leadership, not the best development strategy to offer to the Third World.

Whether the Chinese formula for integrated development is good for everyone, more particularly the developing nations, is a matter of judgment. Although there is no homogeneity within the Third World, China undoubtedly shared many common denominators with underdeveloped countries when it set about its revolution, and it offers at any rate a unique illustration, if not a model, of socioeconomic advancement. Even given the flaws of radical Maoism, China succeeded in banishing abject poverty over the past three decades. How long China will sustain its progress remains to be seen, but its success must depend on making all the factors of integrated development—the social no less than the economic and political—the object of policy. That is a task it shares with the rest of the world.

[15] Dong Furen, Deputy Director of the Institute of Economic Studies at the Chinese Academy of Social Sciences, speaking at a seminar on "China's Economy in the 1980s," Hong Kong, March 1980. *South China Morning Post,* March 8, 1980.

Recent World Development and Its Impact on the Poor in the Third World

ANDRE FRANCO MONTORO
SENATOR, BRAZIL

ONE OF the most important characteristics of world development during the last decades was the economic and political strengthening of the trilateral system integrated by the United States, the European community, and Japan.

In 1976, according to the World Bank's estimates,[1] the United States, the Western European countries, and Japan had 16.2 percent of the world population, 62.1 percent of the world production, and participated with a rate of 63.9 percent in the world export market.[2] Moreover, developing countries[3] with a low income (up to $300 per head) represented 29.3 percent of the population, had only 2.8 percent of the world production, and participated with only 1.9 percent in world exports. In addition, the situation of developing countries with moderate income exceeding $300 per head, though not so grave, was still very different from that of countries in the first group: 25 percent of the population, 14 percent of the production, 20.7 percent of world exports. The contrast was also clearly evident in 1977 when the income per head of the industrial countries which correspond to the trilateral system

---

[1] "Informe sobre el desarollo mundial," 1979 (Washington, D.C., 1979).

[2] In the Eastern countries with an economic system of central planning, the participation in international transactions has been reduced. On the one hand, in 1960, this participation was 12 percent and in 1976 only 9 percent. On the other hand, in 1976, the participation of industrialized countries was 63 percent and that of developing countries only 21 percent. The limitation, as well as the difficulties, in the statistics field explains why this study concentrates on the so-called industrialized and developing countries.

[3] According to the international organizations' criteria, the developing countries can be divided into two groups: countries with a low income and countries with a moderate income.

was $6,980, that of the countries with moderate income $1,140, and that of the countries with low income $170.

In order to have an idea of the strengthening of the macromarket constructed by the economies which constitute the trilateral system, it is enough to remind oneself that transactions among the United States, Western European countries, and Japan during the 1930 decade represented 40 percent of the world market. This proportion grew to 47 percent in 1960 and to 57 percent in 1970. On the other hand, between 1948 and 1970, exchanges in this group of countries increased from 64 percent to 77 percent of its external trade.[4]

THE TRILATERAL COMMISSION

The strengthening of this system has been accompanied by the growth of multinational enterprises whose economic power constitutes one of the most important political forces in the international structure.

The Trilateral Commission was formally constituted in 1973 with a provisional mandate of three years which has already been renewed for two new periods. The commission is composed of about 300 members from the United States, Canada, Western Europe, and Japan who represent a wide spectrum of commercial, financial, political, and cultural interests.

This commission has an executive committee of twenty-nine members, three regional presidents, and three regional offices in New York, Paris, and Tokyo. Its members express their personal points of view but as soon as any of them occupies a governmental post, he gives up his place in the commission. This has happened with President Jimmy Carter and with important European governmental members.

The main objectives of the commission are:
1. To promote joint work of different persons from different sectors of Western Europe, North America, and Japan for the discussion and solution of mutual problems

---

[4] Aldo Ferrer, "La Commission Trilateral y la Proliferacion del Poder Economico International" (Buenos Aires, 1979), p. 10.

2. To make recommendations on key problems concerning the three regions and their relationship with other countries.
3. To draw public attention to these recommendations, especially in the regions integrated in the commission, and as far as possible to obtain positive answers from governments.

The commission meets at the executive committee level and holds plenary sessions with full participation of its members in cities of the three regions in order to examine problems of common interest and particularly to discuss the conclusions of special studies presented by specialists of each region with consultants' help.[5] This formality, combined with the organizational power of big enterprises for activating the international market, explains the multinationals' expansion. They act on a world level while bypassing states' sovereignty. It is sufficient to recall that in 1970, according to authorized calculations, more than 25 percent of world trade was of exchanges within those enterprises.

IMPACT ON THE THIRD WORLD

What are the repercussions of this system on the Third World's development?

The expectancy aided by intensive publicity and changing ideas was that the development of the Third World would be helped and stimulated by means of its integration in the world economic system. But facts presented here have not confirmed these expectations.

The social indexes show an even more grave reality. In 1975, the percentage of literate adults in high-income countries was 99 percent, 69 percent in middle-income countries, and only 36 percent in low-income countries.

[5] Information concerning the Trilateral Commission is taken mainly from *ibid.*, p. 19 ff. and from "Empresas Transnacionales y Transferencia de Technologia," in *Alternativas para una Nueva Ordem Internacional* (CEESTEM, Mexico, 1978) p. 83. On pp. 154 and 160 of this book, one can find a vast bibliography on multinational enterprises.

Life expectancy is seventy-four years in high-income countries, sixty in moderate-income countries, and only fifty in poor countries.

The death rate of children in 1977 was one per 1,000 in high-income countries, 11 per 1,000 in moderate-income countries, and 19 per 1,000 in poor countries. The number of doctors per 10,000 inhabitants is 16, 2, and 1 respectively.

Since the end of World War II, the publicization of these issues which reveal the disparities between countries has made public opinion and international organizations more sensitive to this problem. The constatation that high-income countries are industrialized ones whereas low-income countries are essentially agricultural has led numerous countries to undertake vast industrialization programs on the suggestions and with the help of international organizations.

These programs have been a big success for many countries, as seen from global production value. The World Bank study shows that during 1960–1976 the joint economic performance of these countries, measured by the GNP, had overtaken that of other countries, rich or poor, in global value as well as per capita. Consequently, there was a high rate of growth and industrialization—but who has benefited from this growth?

The following are official statistics. They concern Brazil but they are similar to those found in the group of recently industrialized countries, so-called NIC (newly industrialized countries), where besides Brazil can be found Mexico, Argentina, South Korea, and Taiwan among others which are in the process of incorporating themselves into the same economic type as Venezuela and Colombia in Latin America; Egypt, Nigeria, and Algeria in Africa; Malaysia and the Philippines in Asia.

According to the statistics, during 1963–1979 car production increased by 55 percent, refrigerators by 42 percent, television sets by 41 percent, radios, and phonograph equipment by 89 percent. In contrast, the production of wheat, rice, and beans, which make up the basic diet of the population, has increased by 56.8 percent only, or less than the population's growth, which was 56.9 percent during the same period. In addition, the production of meat has increased even less, precisely 50 percent.

Given that production of cars, refrigerators, television sets, radios, phonograph equipment, and other luxury goods is under the control of powerful multinational enterprises, it is obvious that these countries' development and integration within the world economic system are brought about for the benefit of big enterprises and not to the advantage of the real needs of the population. Generally, the situation in these countries shows that their attachment to the international system has increased their dependence, especially in so far as it has led them to produce and consume not exactly the goods that answer the population's needs (food, clothing, education, decent housing, health), but exactly what represents dominating forces within world economy: cars, refrigerators, radios, television sets, and other superfluous consumer goods. It is consumerism which leads, pressed by the thirst for expansion of big enterprises.

IMPACT ON THE POOR

The impact provoked by this situation on the economy of the Third World countries has been of benefit to the rich and privileged classes of the society which are able to buy luxury goods and disadvantageous to the poorest and most vulnerable groups of the population. These have big difficulties in purchasing food, clothing, medicine, housing, education, and other basic needs.

Development programs based on industrialization followed by these middle-income countries have taken the rich countries' accumulation and consumption as a model. One tried to reproduce as much as possible the production structure of rich countries' economies. This process being a simple copy, has led these countries to be largely dependent on developed centers and to have a high level of external capital participation and external technology that are under the control of multinational enterprises.

It is exactly because of this fact that apart from the characteristic of dependency, this process is marked by an income concentration. So far as the industrialization reproduces a consumer model with high income levels, it is necessary if this model is to be viable that the income of these countries be very concentrated in order to enable the richest classes to buy the high-level goods produced by this industry.

In industrialized countries, the richest 10 percent have 20 percent of the total income of the population, whereas in developing countries the richest 10 percent have about half of the total income. In Sweden, for instance, the richest 10 percent of the population have a per capita income of $19,000, the average income being $9,000; the difference is about two to one. In Brazil, the richest 10 percent have $6,800 dollars per capita, and on the average the population receives only $1,360. The difference is five to one. In contrast, in countries like Mexico, Brazil, and Peru the poorest 40 percent of the population have less than 10 percent of the income that represents less than a quarter of the per capita income in these countries. One should note that since the income in these countries is low in comparison to the income in rich countries, one can conclude that about half of their population is living in poverty.

The income per capita of the minority with high income is equivalent to the income average in developed countries. The other side of the coin is the extreme poverty of the majority of the population and the big income disparities between social strata. In developed countries, the richest receive approximately five times what 40 percent of the poorest receive while in developing countries, the rich receive between fifteen and thirty times more than the poorest 40 percent of the population.

AUTHORITARIAN REGIMES PROMOTE ELITISM

This evident unjust situation was constituted by authoritarian political regimes. Suppression of fundamental freedom, press censorship, control of means of communication, and different modalities of repression have enabled a minority linked to the big national and international interests to impose on developing countries economic models that do not reflect the real aspirations and needs of the majority of the population.

We can even affirm that authoritarianism is the condition for growing elitism. Authoritarian regimes impose solutions and exclude any criticism. The centralization of functions and bureaucracy are the main features of the political model predominant in the Third World.

The sum of powers concentrated in the heads of government has practically suppressed autonomy and vitality in other sectors of national life. States and provinces by their political and financial dependence have been reduced to having only executive functions. Municipalities have lost their financial capacity and the possibility of making decisions on matters of particular concern to them. Workers and even national businessmen are excluded from big decisions of particular concern to them. The voices of representative organizations of agricultural, industrial, and commercial employees are not heard. The autonomy of universities and the acts of the scientific community are limited. Legislative power loses its independence. The means of communication, the theater, the arts, and other aspects of culture are usually controlled. The central government alone dominates and commands; the others can do nothing but obey.

But authoritarianism, centralization, and arbitration do not contribute to the solution of most serious national problems. On the contrary, these problems always become more insupportable for a large portion of the population.

The certainty that real national problems will be resolved by a strong regime is growing in the people's belief more and more. The big aim of the people is to follow the democratic path.

THE PEOPLE'S PARTICIPATION IN DEMOCRACY

However, in many South American countries of the Third World, the old concept of representative democracy is beginning to be substituted or complemented by that of people's participation. In almost all sectors of civilized societies, workers, clerks, neighborhood associations, religious communities, women's movements, professors, students, scientific communities, small and middle-sized enterprises, farmers, artists, consumers, ecologists, defenders of communal autonomy, cooperatives, and other kinds of associations organize themselves and begin to demand active participation in the process of development. They overcome traditional attitudes of indifference and passivity, and each time a much clearer view of their situation and possibilities is attained.

The Cardinal of São Paolo made the following comment to this effect:

People begin to interest themselves in politics. They do not want to be victims, objects, or toys of the political system. They decide to play an active role. But politics do not represent the total range of social relationships. Intermediate organs like trade unions and other associations accomplish their task, which cannot be transferred in the new political reality.

We do not have to build a society only "for the people" but also "with the people."

Among the most important forms of this participation of the community in its conduct of societal life, one can mention:
1. At the local level: residents' or neighborhood associations, community centers, popular movements, mothers' clubs, basic communities
2. At the employment level: trade-union activities, all kinds of participation by employees in enterprise life and in the social development processes
3. At the youth and education level: youth movements, with their organization and participation in school organizations and in discussions on national problems
4. At the political level: the struggle for a democratic structure of parties and for the fundamental right to participate in making decisions, especially in elaborating programs and in choosing candidates
5. Other forms of participation such as associations for environmental protection, cooperatives, consumer associa-

tions, cultural institutions, and other kinds of community organizations.[6]

It is the population which organizes itself to cooperate in the practice of power. It is the substitution of technical "paternalism" for democratic and creative "participation."

All these initiatives are linked to a humanitarian trend which is at the same time individualist and communal. This trend is, on the one hand, opposed to anarchy and dispersive individualism and, on the other hand, to governmental centralization and totalitarianism. The first, under the pretext of defending an abstract "individual" and his liberty, equally abstract, is against institutions and the reinforcement of intermediary associations. On the other hand, state control which concentrates its social powers in the hand of governmental organs dismisses or absorbs the autonomy of these intermediate organizations.

These latter two are obstacles to the natural development of the human being which is normally realized through social groups such as the family, school, district, enterprise, profession, social class, municipalities, and other kinds of genuine communities. It is through these communities that people integrate and participate in the life of the whole society. In this way, one substitutes paternalism for participation.

The paternalist method of action is dictatorship: "Do not think, because the boss will think for you." In the same way, plans implemented without participation of its members are also paternalist. In contrast, social processes are all the processes which stimulate the participation of the population by several forms of organizations and mobilization of the community.

A participating democracy appears to be a political and social pattern able to answer modern needs and offer a new social way of life. This kind of democracy is also able to hinder the imposition of nonappropriate technologies and patrons' patterns and to assure the respect and answer the real needs of the population.

[6] Andre Franco Montoro, "A Luta pela Democracia na America Latina," Brasilia, 1977.

CONCLUSIONS AND PROPOSITIONS

As a summary of this presentation, one can formulate the following conclusions:

1. One of the most important features of world development in the last decades has been the reinforcement of the trilateral system integrated by the United States, the European community, and Japan.

2. This reinforcement has been accompanied by the growth of multinational enterprises whose economic power today constitutes one of the most important political strengths in the international structure.

3. The expectation that the Third World's development would be facilitated and stimulated by its integration in the world economic system has been destroyed by those facts. Reality has shown that this integration has increased dependence in as far as it has led less-developed countries to produce and consume not exactly the goods their populations need but precisely what represents the will and interest of the dominating power in the international system.

4. The impact on the Third World's economy provoked by this situation has been favorable to the rich and privileged classes that are able to purchase luxury goods and to the disadvantage of the poorest and most vulnerable classes who have had difficulties in buying their food, clothing, medications, housing, education, and other basic necessities.

5. Generally, one can see the realization of the process in Third World countries under the emblem of authoritarian regimes where fundamental freedom of the citizen, of the press and other means of communication, censorship and other forms of repression, have facilitated the imposition of economic models that do not reflect the real aspirations and needs of the majority of the population. What are the ways that can modify this situation?

The increasingly clear conscience of Third World populations and the conclusions of their researchers, social workers, and politicians, indicate the following measures as fundamental directions to correct this diversion:

1. At the political level: substitution of authoritarian and centralized regimes by democratic ones with participation of the population or intermediate communities in decisions of local or national interest
2. At the economic planning level: abandonment of development models copied from industrialized centers and their replacement by patterns oriented toward each country's reality and toward the production of goods really necessary for the population
3. At the social level: insurance to all sectors of the population a real and equal participation in development process and results
4. At the cultural plan level: hinder the imposition of values and nonappropriate types of consumption and technology, respect local characteristics, and sustain the artistic creations and technology of each region's population.

It is the only way to prevent exploitation of the human masses by economic groups or the dictatorship oppression. It is the only way to progress toward a real development which favors all mankind.

Let me convey to you, in the same way in which I did in a recent conference for young people in Strasbourg, the three wise lessons from my political experience which can be adapted to people working in the social field.

First, in social fields, as well as in the sciences, mistakes have to be studied and not covered up. It is only discussions and criticism which can overcome deficiencies and promote progress.

Second, in the life of societies, as well as in the natural order, real progress comes from the roots. It is necessary for growth to be like that of trees which receive all their food from the roots.

Finally, if you want to know whether you have chosen the right path in the struggle for justice and liberty, ask yourself: What do the poor think of me?

Millions of people, suffering terrible deprivation and still today not in a position to benefit from civilization, begin to be aware of this forsaken situation of exploitation and oppression and begin to assume the historical role of transforming the process of world development.

It is necessary to understand and support this movement. It is the only way to have development with justice. And it is only in this way that development can become the new name for peace.

People Are the Policy

WILLIAM A. DYSON

EXECUTIVE DIRECTOR, VANIER INSTITUTE OF THE FAMILY, OTTAWA, CANADA

HONG KONG is one of the great hub cities of the planet; here all human strands touch. The East meets the West, the North meets the South. The streets are alive with the many colors and voices of humanity. An international gold market, second only to London's, and an opulence that few of us know are encountered without great difficulty. On the other hand, more readily seen are poverty and marginal life, some of it the most dire.

Here we find family life of great depth and breadth and strength, a kind of family life that is little known these days in the West. In contrast, here also we can find the most rejected and isolated of humanity, human dregs bereft of opportunity, people whose greatest wealth is in the coin of despair. So it is with the "boat people" and many others.

It is a most virile city, a city that offers a future for many, a place to grow, to succeed, to climb higher on the rungs of the planetary social order. It is also the end of a chaotic road for others. It is a great world crossroad's market, where anything and any service are available, including drugs, legal and illegal, on the open and black markets.

Hong Kong is a place of soul-stirring, awesome sunsets of entrancing beauty; it also cowers at times within the terrors of the typhoon that can roar across the islands and the bays. With all its wonders and sorrows, it is us; it is a human crucible.

Perhaps, most of all, it is a city of endurance, tenacity, human ingenuity, and hope. And so it is good that we meet here to consider and reflect upon our development as people who inhabit all corners of the planet.

As I considered the conference theme and reflected upon it, I wondered how we would approach the matter if once again we lived in times when economies were judged to be still sound and producing sufficient surplus to pay for social programs. My guess is that we would keep on doing what we were accustomed to doing, only doing more of it, more of the same.

If nothing else, the uncertainty of the times, therefore, is useful as it gives us pause—even forces us—to reconsider our understanding of, and our approach to, development. And how we regard "development" is crucial to our common future. So let us review briefly some developmental history as it has touched this area of the world.

In contrast to other ancient Asiatic cities, Hong Kong is a new and modern city. Yet, as little as two centuries ago, these islands harbored only fishing villages and pirate havens. In this sense Hong Kong is a symbol of the modern era, a time when access to the whole planet has become a reality and huge and crowded cities have exploded upon the world scene.

While Hong Kong is a place of mixing and meeting for all humankind from all races, it is a place of contradictions. While the predominant people are the Chinese, the skyline and the predominant architecture are clearly modern European. Here we see compounded the tensions and dilemmas that occur when the cultural patterns of a very ancient way of life have imposed upon them the artifacts, whether physical, social, or mental, of another, and very different, way of life.

As we all know, knowledge of any access to all parts of the planet is still recent history. It is only in the times of Columbus and Vasco da Gama in the late 1400s that the sea lanes of the planet were opened up, followed in very recent decades by the air lanes over which most of us today travel. It is only somewhat more than four centuries ago that the first Europeans, the Portuguese and the Dutch, arrived in this region. Nearby Macao was founded only in 1557, bringing the first contacts in this area between a then very new nation, the Portuguese, and a very old civilization, the Chinese. The arrival and impact of the British and the Americans are much more recent, going back less than two centuries.

ASIA AND EARLY WESTERN MODELING

Originally, and it remains true to this day, Europeans came to this part of the world as traders, with imported, loyal, military backing, to support their commercial aggressiveness. Thus the image of ourselves that we from the West projected to those of the East was and is that of commerce, at its best and at its worst. More important, because of its success, especially as industrial, economic, and financial techniques evolved, this way of life became a model, a way to do it, a way to be.

At first, the modeling was unconscious. Rather it was projected through a brand of arrogant brashness that only a people who were the *nouveaux-arrivés* on the world scene could assume—that their way of life was the only way of life and, of course, the best possible. Before the last century ended, the modeling had become more deliberate as commercial growth and financial success were clearly perceived to lie along this path.

As one could expect, the world of commerce entrained other impositions. Western models of government and public administration were to be found by 1900 in India, Indonesia, Indochina, and other smaller pockets like Hong Kong. Modern European military techniques and modes of warfare also were imported. Similarly, and perhaps more subtly, pervasively, and widespread, were the inroads of European models of education, the introduction of its mental processes, whether at the primary level or through universities and their faculties of higher learning.

Only Japan had successfully resisted foreign footholds and dominance in those earlier times. Rather, biding its time, it absorbed the ways of the West on its own terms and did so most successfully. Today it is a world industrial power, the only non-European member nation of the Organization for Economic Cooperation and Development in Paris, a leader, for instance, in the electronics industry with products ranging from high-tech computer components to pachinko games. Yet, strangely, Japan, the most resistant and conservative, has become in recent decades one of the most fully developed countries, in industrial terms, in the world.

But let us backtrack a moment.

CURRENT WESTERN DEVELOPMENT MODELS

As World War II was closing, the great issues of reconstruction in the devastated regions of the world rose to the fore. While there had been some conceptual and theoretical work on national development arising out of the League of Nations in the 1930s, as in the work of Ragnor Nurshe, the real effort began in the Netherlands in 1944 as its economic planners, under Jan Tinbergen, began working out postwar reconstruction developmental schemata. Their work, excellent on its own terms, became the model and the forerunner. All over the West and within the newly established United Nations in the later 1940s and 1950s it led people to work out concrete, high-impact, national and international economic, and, later, social development policies and programs of many kinds and varieties.

At this point, in recent history, the concept of development—deliberate, staged development—appeared and gained a beachhead in human endeavor. No longer were we going to improve ourselves and our nations by accident, by trial and error, or by simple intuitive response. Rather, we would think out and implement our development, using rational, planned methods and practices. Needless to say, "the economy" was assumed to be and was posited as "the engine of development." This approach has become totally dominant, one that is powerful and all-pervasive today and is at the root of our conference deliberations. This assumption is embedded in the conference theme; as such, I aim to place it under attack.

To come to my initial main point: development as now perceived and practiced in most of our countries is both a shibboleth and an aberration. It is worse than a sacred cow; it is a bull that has run wild in the pottery shop. The time has come to stop and take a cold, sober look at it; to take a look at ourselves in the industrialized nations; at whom we in the West have become, and where such models are leading those who come from other regions of the planet.

That all men should eat sufficiently every day is not at issue. Nor is our need for learning, for useful and meaningful work. Nor is our need for human love, caring, support, and commitment. But, I ask, is the present mode of development the only mode, the best mode, the appropriate human mode, even a good one? On all counts I say resoundingly, it is not. And so, I wish to shift our very perspective on the conference theme—to go in another direction, to offer a radical alternate view and approach as we prepare to go about our various courses of action.

To begin, actual Western-type development which has been and is the model offered to the developing nations for over thirty-five years did not begin thirty-five years ago. The evolution of Western development began centuries ago. All prior evolution is assumed when we look at the stages it was and is at in twentieth-century terms. Though glossed over, those earlier centuries of development were and remain a necessary set of stages or components in the *de facto* development of our industrialized nations in the West.

Modern Western industrial development, and the shape of its concommitant modern production, consumption, and service delivery systems, rests on one glaring factor that no one whom I know has yet been able to consider, face, or articulate. This factor is the destruction of community. As our system and our societies now falter and sag, we are learning the cost of this road to development.

The destruction of community. A very ancient and still very fundamental human fact, its roots lost in the mists of prehistory, is that man survived and developed on this planet because he was not alone. He depended upon and needed his fellows whether in his hamlet, his village, his neighborhood, or within his family. Utter mutual interdependence was the basis of life and growth. It has been so for hundreds of thousands of years, and remains so to this very day.

But in the West, "human community," the long-term condition for human survival and growth, was severely damaged with the advent of the dispossessing agricultural reforms of the late Middle Ages. In the immediate centuries to follow, in a variety of forms, it created a rootless mass. This stage of our development was complex and was also linked to new models of knowledge called "science," from which were derived our technologies, and from new modes of work called "employment," from which we derive our "labor force." Together they provide the basis of our mass production. In these basic shifts, we begin to see the early stages of European-type modern development.

Thus the real price that the West paid for its modern societies—and this fact is now coming home to roost—was the destruction and loss of "community." This is so whether we define community as our immediate face-to-face environment or as the extended family and neighborhood people networks that for millenniums had been the solid foundation of all human experience and life. No longer was the natural group important. Under the myth, the individual person was made king, every man's home became his castle. The way of life that evolved was oriented to strengthening the individual's capacities—the individual seen now as separate from others—especially those capacities oriented to earning more and more so that he could consume more and more and more, and amass more and more and more. In its crudest yet most prevalent terms, this way of life is epitomized today in the well-known phrase in the English-speaking world: "Screw you Charlie, get off my turf."

Social security and the loss of human relationship. In our search for security—it now may be said, perhaps, in our mad search for security—we in the West, by and large, have structured the basic social strengths and capacities right out of our people and out of our industrial way of life. Our social security and social service programs hence are largely artificial, inadequate constructs that try, so far unsuccessfully, to replace the loss of community. We became an uncaring people.

We now construct social security programs because we have lost our old way of life that provided natural social security, a social security found in people close to us. In this is a lesson to be pondered and examined well as those in the East look to the West to provide models of social development. In creating freedom from hunger and want, in our fashion, we have created a vast complex of dependencies whether among the rich, the poor, or those in between, through which we seek to replace the human community, and never will, whether by governmental and/or corporate and/or labor union programs. These extensive dependencies have now trapped us. This wide-scale, long-term cultural process, in full flower in the 1960s, has now peaked, and a general deterioration in Western nations has set in over the last two decades. Fortunately, we are dimly realizing this, and an as yet vague but beginning search for a better, more human life style, a better way of life, is now getting under way in Western nations.

The end result of this process of development was not just the loss of "community"; even deeper was the loss of "wholeness." The world of psychic and spiritual realities was separated out and downgraded. The world of work fragmented people from their homes, from their neighborhood life, from contact and relationship with nature itself. In a new form, the law of the jungle took over and was endowed with the cloak of quasi-scientific virtue apparent in such phrases as Darwin's "survival of the fittest." This new mindset narrowed the rich range of "human enterprise" down to a mode now known as "free enterprise," which in turn opened the road to human greed and unbridled competition that, as we are now learning, are poor substitutes for human collaboration.

In effect, the Western industrial way of life is founded on a cultural form that, in its first unstated early stages, debased the worth of close or intimate human relationships. It has equally debased those necessary human qualities, those normal aspects of daily life, such as caring, sharing, and cooperation and has turned them into saccharine virtues to be tolerated from the mouths of do-gooders such as people like us, who are here to consider social welfare matters.

And so today we have arrived at a point in our parts of the planet when we of the West stuff our mouths with unbelievable and very unhealthy amounts of calories while our factory and bodily eliminations pollute our rivers, lakes, and seas to dangerous and critical levels. Our economies and monies are severely inflated and debased with no end in sight. Our marriages and families fall apart at intolerable rates. Our youth and aged have become a rootless crowd of little worth. Our basis for community, for close, viable human relationships, at whatever level, has been critically hurt.

Why is this so?

THE WESTERN MINDSET AND ITS EFFECTS

THE WESTERN MIND

It is in the nature of all human beings, as they evolve as a tribe or as a people, to interpret reality to themselves in a way that lets them survive and work out common shared living patterns that, taken as a whole way of life, we call a culture. So it was with the peoples of Europe.

In its origins, "development," as expressed in the conference theme, is a Western concept, now nuanced, of course, by many other cultures. It is well based in a concept of futurity and clearly implies the possibility of and the actualization of change. It is expressed simply in the statement, "Today we can change, so tomorrow will be better." It is also well associated with the concept of "growth," more particularly growth narrowly understood and limited to increasing our money, goods, and services. We also expect to see the general availability of these expanding continuously without limit over time. The assumption is one of infinite material increase and growth, as if we were all gods. Asiatic and Oriental as well as African and Amerindian cultures generally chose other routes, evolving different mentalities.

To place the concept of development in context I must talk about the West, about Western industrialized man, whatever his variations, whether in Europe, North America, Australia, or elsewhere. As that maxiculture has touched people on this planet just about everywhere, I am sure that those from non-Western lands will recognize elements of it that have been grafted onto, or are being absorbed into, their own culture and their own way of life.

Western civilization generally had its take-off point in ancient Greece three to four thousand years ago—a late start compared to the cultures of present-day China and India. In that cultural cradle in the Eastern Mediterranean we made our first but lasting separations of tangible and material realities from intangible and immaterial realities—as we say, physics from metaphysics. Here lie the roots whereby we split our physical and material realities away from our human realities. That split is yet today viable and powerful when we remember that it is this split, with which all of us at this conference live at home, in respect to matters of economic policy (material policy) and social policy (people or intangible policy).

Through the modes of what we describe as Aristotelian syllogistic methods of exploring, describing, classifying, and interpreting reality, we learned to separate realities of every kind, one from another, into what have become myriad sub-banks of knowledge, each with numerous branches or specialties. In the course of this cultural evolution, many side effects occurred over the millennium that have made us in the West largely what we are today.

The first side effect was that different realities became separated and fragmented from one another with no binding principle. We see this very evidently in the cross-purposes at which so many well-intentioned people now work.

A second effect is that as each distinction was made, and a contrasting reality differentiation was made, one (unconsciously) was interpreted as superior to, or dominant over, or to be preferred to, the other. For example, boys are seen as better than girls; blonds are better than brunets; "having" is better than "being"; material growth is more important than spiritual growth; science is more essential than philosophy; sociology is less important than chemistry; it is better to be a manager than a worker; housework is less important than office work; factory workers are more important than farmers; and so on. As a result, the downgraded half of each split became lessened in value in our culture, in our very daily way of life—even in our public policies and programs. It sometimes became even invisible, or taken for granted and just used, or simply forgotten, as in the case of parenting, or the day-to-day household activities of women, or the central supportive function of the family in any national developmental plans.

With the Age of Enlightenment and the rise of modern science, material reality clearly came to dominate. Thus a third key side effect of this new cultural stream was that numbers became paramount and numbers became the ultimate criterion of truth. All of us know phrases such as, "You can't argue with the budget"; "That's what the statistics say"; "If you can't measure it, it isn't relevant."

In Western industrial societies every man, woman, and child is numbered, frequently many times over, and is both found and lost in the numbers. Much of the countless wealth of the human attributes of these people and the uncountable qualities of their work and life activities have been made largely invisible and are badly underaccounted for. People and their qualities have been made less than they are. Despite this downgrading, it is well to consider that it is probably because of these countless qualities, strengths, initiatives, and inputs that Western industrial societies are enabled today to carry on, though limping, rather than collapsing outright under the pressure of current system breakdowns. To borrow the jargon of economists, the so-called externalities are carrying the load.

The outcome of this cultural orientation to development has of course been colossal for the West itself. Technological wonders abound in modern physics, medicine, telecommunications, or whatever. People generally are well fed, housed, schooled, and so on, despite relative inequities in our nations. But the guarantees to this fortunate scene are now fast eroding.

This drive for material security has brought about some horrendous planetary imbalances, which means we must do it differently. The peoples of the West are only 20 percent of the earth's population, yet we consume 80 percent of the planet's production. Some of us consume as many as 10,000 calories a day. Americans and Canadians, comprising about 5 percent of the planet, consume slightly over 50 percent of the world petroleum output. Distortions at this level of severity simply will have to ease or we will all crash together. It takes no predictive powers to know that these imbalances are going to come to an end, one way or another, and will do so sooner rather than later.

Equally bad, but less apparent, is what the Western peoples are doing to themselves. For example, we are so oriented to technological growth and expansion, which at first involved harnessing the energy and labor of the adult population, that, no longer needed, we are now leaving a growing and appreciable minority of these people "lying fallow"—we now call them the unemployed, when the correct term is the displaced. This new phenomenon is simply the straight-line dynamic that follows from the technological transfer of work from men to machines to robots.

AN ERA IS ENDING

The Chinese people, it is said, have traditionally thought in terms of five generations. Westerners are just the opposite. Many, if not most of us, live from paycheck to paycheck; or if in business, from sales boom to sales boom; or if in government, from term to term of office. We would find it hard to recognize an epoch if we saw one, let alone the end of one.

We really are quite capable:

1. We walk upon the moon and thank God for system redundancy.
2. Our vehicles circle Mars and send us pictures of awesome sandstorms across millions of miles of space.
3. We explore the ocean floor, and ships drill down through the depths of the earth's crust and on to the Moho.

We of the West are equally a strange people:

1. We pollute the air, block sight of the stars, while our radio stations announce precise pollution measurements of the various poisons we breathe.
2. We also pollute our lakes, rivers, streams, and oceans.
3. We also pollute our ears and metabolisms.

And in so doing:

1. We gobble up our natural resources.
2. We manipulate the chromosomes and are now learning to play new and frightening music on the genetic scale.
3. We pursue a rising standard of living, a standard, a judgment, based solely on a count of our material possessions, while we watch the quality of life slide away from our somewhat indifferent, somewhat grasping fingers.

We have used our capacities in a lopsided fashion.

Our national governments, which reflect us all too well, establish regional economic development plans that further deteriorate our poorer regions; manpower policies that make us more and more subservient to machine policies; welfare policies that undermine the well-being of people; agricultural policies that ruin ordinary farmers, while stored wheat rots and stockpiled butter turns rancid; housing and land policies that increase housing prices faster than incomes; tax reforms that are not tax reforms, no matter what one's viewpoint; resource development policies that deplete and desolate the land and deny us and our children our common patrimony; expensive health policies that cure us faster but do little to make us healthier or happier; educational policies that train more of us for nonexistent jobs and all of us for a world that used to be. This approach to life simply cannot last much longer.

We have done this, so we think and say, in order to "develop," to bring solutions to bear on crucial problems. And our problems, with each so-called solution, get worse. And we dare to offer this to the poorer lands as the way to go.

The rip-off world. It is a world, a way of being in the world, that our young have too aptly named "the rip-off world." It is a world of throwaway gum wrappers, throwaway cars, throwaway city centers, throwaway water, throwaway forests, throwaway houses, even a world of throwaway people. And we are unaware of what we are doing and whom we have become.

Neither capitalist nor socialist economics in the West, despite the best intentions embedded in each, offer any solution. Said simply, they offer only two different styles, two variations on the same approach to seeing the world. In their present institutionalized forms they are both geared to an ever-expanding vicious circle of unknowing and uncaring, exploitative production and consumption of goods and services. Both are but variations on the basic theme of Western man—to despoil the earth and its bounty. Both chase a rising material standard of living and both suffer not only from its resultant despoliation but more seriously from very severe social dislocations.

The good life, illusion or reality? To illustrate, all the so-called strong and developed nations promise the improverished Third World the good life, as if there were now present on earth sufficient metals, oil, and materials of all kinds to match the current high Western standards. It is physically impossible that every family, whether in the United States, Canada, Russia, China, India, Japan, Indonesia, Nigeria, Angola, Brazil, Bolivia, and so on, shall some day have two cars, a town house, and a cottage in the country, apart from umpteen refrigerators, stoves, home computers, radios, color television sets, automatic dishwashers, and electric martini mixers. We all need to come down to earth.

Nor can we leave nature aside from this unwitting world dynamic. We of the Western nations have sought for centuries to dominate nature, to force it into submission. We have felt free to exploit it widely and we still do so. Apart from the needs of later generations, nature herself has begun to react, to bite back, to force upon us an awareness of her abiding presence and of her ways. She is reducing us to size. She is doing so in some very heavyhanded ways too. The Atlantic grows into a cesspool of human wastes, petroleum, and endless debris. Our polluted air increases our weather inversions, our respiratory diseases, and deaths. Acid rain blights our lakes and forests. Our drinking water grows guckier. Our biosphere is heating up. Our insects swarm, and natural biota cycles and chains are broken and destroyed. Our cut-over land erodes. No, nature has not been idle. Yet the more our science studies it, the less do we know it, let alone respect it.

And people in the West are beginning to realize that things are somehow wrong.

NOISE IN THE ECHO CHAMBER

People are communicating their questions, fears, dissent, and anger in odd ways, whether through divorce, strikes, or terrorism.

The less industrialized nations signal the times through OPEC (Organization of Petroleumn Exporting Countries).

People are communicating, though the means are not the normal political channels. But, below these events, the general malaise runs deep. Alienation and a sense of indifference seep across our lands, and hope withers on the part of the governors and the governed alike.

These foibles and inconsistencies have accumulated and multiplied and ramified so deeply into and through our lives that people ask, "Is the world mad or is it me?" or say, as many do, "Stop the world; I want to get off!"

What is happening? How did we Westerners become this way?

The whole cloth of life. Clearly, all of it is not unconnected. Whether it be pollution, political disorder, resource depletion, rising divorce rates, nuclear brinkmanship, urban swarm and deterioration, inflation, social unrest, unemployment—it is all part of the same cloth. Each can be seen as a symptom of an underlying dynamic, a syndrome inherent in the general culture.

In each and every instance, the events are speaking to us about how people think, feel, and behave today, whether at home, at work, at school, at church, at play. They manifest a set of attitudes, a social outlook in respect to one's own life and life in the world about us generally.

In this sense all of these matters—economic, political, cultural, spiritual, scientific, and so on—have a broad and deep people dimension, a broad and deep social dimension. In the context of today's realities, to discuss policy outside that dimension is to joust at windmills. To tackle the so-called people-problems later, after we have settled the real issues, such as money, is to stumble further into the already widespread loss of faith in governmental solutions. To tackle people issues the way we do now, under the rubrics of welfare, manpower retraining, social services, corrections, youth programs, work incentives, and all such illusory policies, is to tackle only the surface symptoms and to force ourselves more surely into a dead end.

WHERE LIES SANITY?

Our capacity for physical accomplishment is no longer in question. No longer is the issue what we can do. It is why we do it.

The deeper underlying issue is what capacity do we have for social accomplishment—to make life, as we live it daily, better for all of us, whether back home in Ottawa, whether here in Hong Kong and all its neighborhoods, or in the various regions of the world. That something is wrong, that something profound is happening, that we need to become a different kind of people, is being voiced more and more consciously. We need only reflect upon the recent North-South dialogues on a new world economic order; or upon *North-South,* the report of the Commission on International Development.[1] Or listen to the words of Pope John Paul II as he traveled in Brazil in June of 1980. Yet we in the policy and program fields, social and otherwise, whether as "policy advisors" or as program and field workers, behave as if our policy work and programs were real, as if the noisy world outside was but a passing illusion, just static in the system.

Most of us have grown to believe that everyone knows what's real, that reality is a "given," that it is something we can take for granted just as we can count on the sun to rise and set every single day. But is this really so?

Many people believe in going to church—many don't. Many people believe that a woman's place is in the home—many don't. Many people believe that in science lies our salvation—many don't. Many people believe in capitalism—many don't.

[1] *North–South: a Program for Survival,* **Report of the Independent Commission on International Development Issues under the chairmanship of Willy Brandt (London: Pan Books, 1980).**

Many people believe in the use of force—many don't. Many people believe in long hair—many don't. Many people believe in competition—many don't. Many people believe in a unified world—many don't. Many people believe in sexual freedom—many don't.

The list today has become endless.

A world of many realities. What is real and right and true and good for me may, or may not, be the same for you. Often we differ today, not only among provinces or countries, but among members of the same household. Yet we all want to hold realities in common; for therein lies any stability to go forward, therein lies any tomorrow. But it is clear that such is not the case at present; we live in a world that is a jungle of realities where each of us is striving to survive, to keep sane, to remain human.

However, a fundamental lesson lies in recognizing that realities differ. If there are so many realities, then "reality" is not "a given," it is not absolute, it cannot be taken for granted. Clearly, reality is relative, it can vary and shift; it always has and always will. But if we can come to understand reality in this way, we see that we can choose our realities *consciously* rather than accepting them unconsciously out of training, indoctrination, or habit, as we now do.

It also becomes clear that our common reality is something we, as individual persons, as a nation, as a race, invent and build over time. Over the years, through our own daily training, habits, understandings, small and big choices and decisions, each of us builds his or her own reality. Where it becomes widely shared, it can become a new culture.

A TIME TO GO BEYOND

When we believed that the world was flat, exploration and transport by sea were severely constrained. Only as that "reality" gave way, only when men could go beyond that reality in their minds and guts, could they venture out physically and deliberately, and actually go beyond, go on to greater experiences, on to wider and richer realities.

In the course of history there came times to examine our reality and to go beyond it to another, to a richer reality. Let me illustrate.

In the geometry that we have all been taught, we learned that the angles of any triangle total 180° and that the shortest distance between any two points is a straight line. That is Euclidian geometry, and we still use it to build bridges, houses, even to cross the street. But the two propositions are sometimes true and sometimes they are not.

Applying triangulation to the earth as a sphere we find, for instance, that two longitudinal lines joined at the poles which then cross the equator, each cross the equator at 90°. The two angles so formed, twice 90°, equal 180°; and adding that third angle at the pole makes it 180° plus that angle. The same is true if one quarters half an orange. And so there are triangles bigger than 180°.

That is why when we look at a map that illustrates a ship crossing from New York to London, Sydney to Valparaiso, or Vancouver to Yokohama, that ship will be on a curved line. The same is true on a flight map from, say, San Francisco to Manila, or from Rome to Nairobi. The shortest distance on a sphere is a curved line. This, oversimplified, of course, is Riemannian geometry, worked out by a forerunner of Einstein. It is based on spherical objects and not on the flat, planar understandings to which Euclid was limited. Each time we fly or sail long distances today we count on our navigator knowing this "beyond-Euclid" mathematics. If he didn't, traveling would be as dangerous as it used to be. We also use it to place all our satellites up; spatial ballistics use imaginary circles in the sky, and that is how a satellite gets placed on a course to stay in orbit, go to the moon, or go to Mars.

What is important in this example is that sometimes a reality taken to be the whole thing is not enough. Sometimes it holds and at other times it does not. If one reality is insufficient or constraining, it is time to seek a fuller, richer understanding that goes beyond. This is what we need to do today. This is the challenge. It is time to go beyond on "goods and services" and go to people.

CONFLICTING REALITY PATTERNS—A TIME TO CHOOSE

While there are many realities, and the full reality of no one of us is exactly the same as someone else's, nevertheless there are widely shared broad patterns. Analysis shows that people from Western nations generally tend to live not by a single shared pattern, but by three quite different sets. These three mindsets, or world outlooks, or attitude patterns, or understandings of reality sets, are derived from differing perceptions of the world, often out of the same kinds of phenomena which we perceive differently under different circumstances and under differing outlooks. Out of these reality views, out of these sets of perceptions, flow our value sets. The constellations of our value sets vary also from one mindset to another, so that some perceptions are valued highly under one light, less so under another, or are rejected outright under another. And here lies the source of much of our conflict today in the West about where to go and how to do it.

Briefly, these three outlooks can be described as:
1. The clockwork world of the megamachine
2. The humanistic yet highly individualistic world
3. The organic world of human interrelationship.

A SHARED REALITY: STANDARDIZED, REPLACEABLE MAN

All reality is defined by opposing categories whereby superior values are set. Moreover, once a definition is set, once more and more phenomena or events about us can be converted to possessing similar attributes, reality is considered easier to handle. Thus we begin to establish standards and norms to fit what we now—or at any given time or period of history—perceive as good or better. This leads from standards to standardizing, where we seek to make the phenomena uniform, to make it conform to our perceptions of reality. Thus we grade coal and build machines to break it down to more or less uniform sizes. We do the same with petrol, using octanes as the norm. We have used standardizing in the past to convert people to a prescribed religion; today we use it for quasi-religious political beliefs; for grading school children, for instance, through IQ or social performance scales; we use it at work, through job descriptions, job definitions, and job evaluation scales; in government, through standardizing and normalizing regulations built into any legislated program. Just as reality gets squeezed into molds, in the same way are people also forced into preconceived molds, whether they fit or not.

But to do this some other things also had to happen, and still do. The very process of definition is built on a process of exclusion. Once we define something as a car we exclude it from being a cart or a wagon. And the more heavily we define anything, each additional definition or categorization excludes more and more. With the result by reduction we arrive at highly specialized definitions, which exclude and make invisible a host of other related data. Thus, with a man defined as a worker, we do not take into account that he is also a husband, father, churchgoer, party member, sports fan, and so on. When it comes to job performance, all that is usually excluded.

In this fashion through classification we reduce all reality to comparable, recognizable, manageable, uniform units. And every nonincluded attribute is thereby automatically devalued. In this fashion we organize all such reality in our heads and then, so we believe, organize the world about us into a smoothly functioning system, the excluded data having dropped from view.

Thus we define and organize our land, our metals, our products and services—even our people. If any part of this organized system fails to fulfill the norms established for it, it can be replaced by another comparable, uniform unit, whether it be an alternator in a car, a rheostat in a stage lighting system, a chair seat in a kitchen set, a transistor in a radio or space capsule relay—or a plumber, a clerk, a nuclear engineer, a company president, an undersecretary, a school janitor, a high school student, a clergyman, or a radio operator. Each is a replaceable unit, having been refined and reduced from its original material whether iron, tree, copper, air, water, or flesh and blood. We have equated people to replaceable machine parts, and our models of social organization are machinelike. Accordingly, we seek to scale down everything and everyone to a simple time-and-space unit. The purpose is to have everything and everyone in the right place, at the right time, doing the right thing, in the right way. In this world of reality perception, everything, *including every person*, is viewed, valued, and treated as an object, as a thing.

The clockwork world has had great impact on the family in the industrialized nations, reducing its extension, reducing it to its nuclear form. This familial form, built on reductive roles instead of persons, more easily manipulable for industrial purposes, is probably the most fragile and vulnerable form of familial life in human history. Its rate of breakdown is now epidemic.

Alongside this cultural thought train lie other related and reinforcing processes to handle reality in this way, such as objectification, reification, quantification, and mechanization.

A SYSTEM OF "ITS"

Early in our long Western history we split our heads from our guts. In seeking to define and handle reality we found it easier to turn everything into objects outside ourselves. In doing this, we downgraded what was subjective, what dealt with feelings, emotion, and human response. As a result a large world of reality was and is largely excluded from our perceptions, and from priority in our values, and thereby given little or no attention in the public domain. We became passionate in our search to be dispassionate. It was an ideal of science.

Moreover, as we objectified the world, it became apparently easier to evaluate it by counting the objects—how much coal, how much oil, how many cars; how many dollars, yen, rubles, and so on; how many workers, how many schools, how many believers—all built on tangibles. Joy and satisfaction became measured in days away from work, frequency of sex, ounces of alcohol, number of rooms in a house, marks at school. Our goals are also quantified whether it be x growth, dollars budgeted, number of people "helped," "taught," and the like. Qualities, always less tangible, we found harder to judge and evaluate, and so judgments of quality declined as a value, as a daily method, as a priority, and a world of measurement took over.

And objects being still easier to handle, we turned certain ideas and concepts also into objects, such as "national development." As a result we pursue it as if it too were a material object, a goal, and seek to increase "it," to have "more." Some people will even say they can and will build a measurement scale of this "moreness"; they promise to quantify national development. This is why we now chase "social indicators" just at a time when economic indicators, such as the GNP, are increasingly regarded as mythical and are starting to lose their sacred status.

Thus all reality—people, nature, ideas—has become "its." As things, all can be supposedly manipulated. As "its" all are reduced and therefore can be exploited to favor the system, the machine that we plan to build for ourselves as our better world.

Through the same process, a supposedly responsible government can throw away jobs and workers (people and their activity) as if they were simply excess inventory to stave off more inflation (a cancer in the system) by sticking Band-aids on a creaking, dead-end type of economy. To be sure, not only governments, but most of us in the West tend to place "systems" first in any crunch. People come last. And it is on this basis that we of the West judge "development" whether of nations, of regions, of people such as our neighbors, even of ourselves. We all participate in this machine view of reality, seeking various statuses and labels (opposing categorizations), objectively ascertained, properly graded, ranked, and costed (quantified), placing such labels on all sorts of things, including ourselves.

But the full impact of this mode of seeing all reality is an attempt, now becoming dysfunctional even futile, to order and control it all—us too—so that the system and its various subsystems will all function well. Thus we use all kinds of methods to order groupings, whether they be parts in a machine, units in a school, a factory, a government office, a city, a country, an alliance group, a world. Thus each of us is seen in theory and practice to be part of a system, of an engine, relating to other engines, all adding up to a hoped-for, some day, well-running superengine called megamachine.

Such is the epistemological basis of almost all of what we today call "organization," "coordination," and "planning," whether economic or social, no matter under what ideology. In contrast, though, what seems to be now happening is that a host of excluded phenomena, whether personal, human, qualitative, organic, natural, rhythmic, or subjective—all called "problems"—have now risen to haunt us. So heavy is their impact that the world now rattles.

A RICHER, YET NARROW FAMILIAL REALITY

A second way that we all perceive reality is personal. It is usually created in the family. This is an outlook we learn at home. With it we perceive the humanness of members of the family, friends, close working colleagues, and unsystematized peers. We tend to see every such person in a whole way, valuing each person for his own self with his own particular talents, qualities, and weaknesses. Love, grief, joy, anger, fun, pain, and pleasure all are present and dealt with. Growth is recognized as rhythmic, not scheduled; home and garden are cared for, not exploited; people and their differences tend to be tolerated, if not cherished and nurtured; idiosyncrasy is better accepted; success and failure are evaluated differently; moral issues are recognized as such; self-identity and not blind uniformity is given some importance; give-and-take and selflessness are sought for and frequently found; qualities are seen and nurtured and evaluated as such.

Today, "family" as we perceive it, is rather narrowly focused. We aim to look after *our* family first. Our property is *our* property and guarded as such. For instance, we don't dump our garbage on the lawn or flush our toilets into the swimming pool, but we don't mind if they are dumped into our common fields, rivers, and seas. And while we are very human at home, it is an individualistic humanism directed to our own good. We generally leave it behind once we cross our own doorstep and enter the outside world. Once there again, we tend to relate to one another as systematized roles and functions. This individualistic aspect shows up clearly when we take our humanism out of the house.

For many decades now, through values based in this familial, humanistic mindset, we have sought to humanize the world. It has been and still largely is the source of the values of our reform movements. Unfortunately, the methods such movements use are grounded in those of the clockwork, mechanistic world. Thus the unperceived reality, the world outlook in which the methods of our various "power" movements and human rights movements are imbedded, is a debased humanism, one hobbled by the same clockwork, mechanistic techniques as the rest of our public activity.

HUMAN RIGHTS, A CLOCKWORK CONCUBINE

The linkage between these two mindsets, these two views of reality, is nowhere better seen than in our concept of "work," especially the right to work. Work in the clockwork world is any human activity recognized in general as meriting a money payment, and specifically as actually legitimated by payment of the money. It is called "employment." But we all know deep down that a person out of work, unemployed, does not disappear, even though statistically he is off the so-called labor market. Instead, while some become depressed and inactive, the so-called unemployed person may well be repairing his house or car, studying, organizing a welfare rights group, hunting, meditating, fishing, making a bomb in the cellar, growing vegetables, talking to and helping some aged or sick person—all of which is "work," but not "employment." Thus we live "officially" by an illusion. No country is short of work in fact or in potential. Rather, it is short of "employment," which is nothing more than an artificial construct of reality and therefore changeable.

Similarly, a third of all adults who are active are defined not even as "unemployed" but as invisible nonpersons so far as the labor market is concerned, that is, the billion or more women who "just" raise children and "just" keep house. All of them and their work are utterly crucial to our well-being as persons and as a people in each of our homelands. Again, we detect a social and economic illusion, despite efforts to improve the status of women.

Such illusions flow out of our tendency to focus on the narrowly defined "included" phenomena that go on about us. It is time to seek out what we exclude and whom we exclude and to focus on these. For these reasons, labor force and similar statistics are but a modern mumbo jumbo, an incantation to a dying idol, an all-but-gone scientism.

It is out of these two linked and illusory sets of attitudes that come such inane and useless measures as manpower programs aimed essentially at assisting the systems (industry, commerce, governmental agencies, the professions) and not primarily to assist people. This is, in the long term, why laws and programs based on "human rights" attain but empty justice, why unemployment insurance programs become a social illusion playing games to expand aggregate fund income, and then paying people to go away.

This is the world that leads us to a commendable Brandt report. It seeks human development and social justice for all. But with its humanism based in mechanistic modes of reform, it offers no real breakthrough.

WHOLENESS

A third way in which we perceive the world is now becoming more and more apparent and widespread in the West. In the poorer nations, it has had long and valuable roots which are yet visible though they are being attenuated.

For long years, a few have always rejected the clockwork reality imposed upon us. As long ago as 1829, Lord Macaulay wrote clearly on the clockwork world, which he then saw emerging and which is now in full flower. Today a slow recognition seeps in upon us in the West. Fortunately a new, yet quite old and long-submerged, world view is growing once again, as well documented by Marilyn Ferguson in *The Aquarian Conspiracy*.[2]

It is a world view wherein we tend to perceive all reality as

[2] Marilyn Ferguson, *The Aquarian Conspiracy* (New York: Tarcher, 1980).

interrelated, in contrast to the clockwork world which fragments and separates it and us. Some would call this third view an "ecological" view, a "holistic" view, a "relational" view, an "organic" view, an all-encompassing way of perceiving the world about us. It is a world of interrelationship that Réné Dubos now talks about.

Its keynote is general recognition and respect for all persons and cultures as well as recognition and respect for nature itself. All are seen in a symbiotic relationship, all are interdependent. Its central concept is best expressed, though poorly, by "community." We extend what we learn in the family to a broader family, ultimately to all people everywhere. The world itself is perceived as "home."

It enables us to see science, though important, as only one form of knowing. We come to value a variety of ways of knowing, whether through insight, intuition, or experience. We join mind and feeling, recognizing that all decisions, whether admitted or not, whether at home, in board rooms, or cabinet offices, ultimately are, for good or ill, gut decisions as well as head decisions. It does not let us escape the recognition that all decisions, including research decisions, are moral decisions. Cooperation is placed ahead of competition, so that broader contexts of agreement are sought to contain and resolve the conflicts that life inevitably brings.

It lets us recognize body as well as soul and lets us rejoice in their oneness, in their expansiveness, acknowledging pain as well as joy. Being is valued over doing, becoming over finalizing. Doing is more humanly purposive and occurs in the context of the quality of life.

Technology, as complex as it is, is seen as nothing more or less than an extension of man, yet as such, important. The aim is to bring it under man's direction, so that like any human tool or instrument it can serve man, not enslave him.

We are led to nurture and cherish what we have, to conserve it, to use it well, not to exploit it or suppress it blindly, whether it be our human spirit, our capacities, our land, our wealth, our resources.

This outlook explains why many people in the industrialized

nations are now beginning to reject openly our mechanistic way of life. For instance, I note the movement in Norway called "The Future Is in Our Hands." This world view explains why many Asiatics, Latin Americans, and Africans seek another route, since they have always lived more closely to that way of seeing and being in the world.

Thus, without realizing it, in varying degrees we all live by three mindsets: a clockwork, megamachine view of the world; a humanistic but highly individualistic view; and a view of all reality, us included, existing in an organic, interdependent relationship. As we go from one life context to another, we shift mindsets automatically, almost as if we shifted from one set of lens to another to see life about us, few of us recognizing that we do so.

The megamachine view, we all know, dominates our public life together and as such controls the Western world, capitalist, socialist, and Communist alike. It tends to control our churches, our schools, our professions, wherever we are supposed to come together as people. This mode of life is no conspiracy. It is just us. It has taken us centuries to shape our current realities and ourselves. All of us perceive and behave in these ways. As such our institutions merely reflect us and we them. We are thus largely unaware and unknowing.

And so, where do we go, whom do we become in our differing nations? The question touches us as people, in our daily lives as well as in our policy-making. It requires a new awareness of our mentalities; it requires another view of development, a common one adapted to the industrialized lands as well as to those which are not.

All continents are mapped. Men are now upon them, including Antarctica, for we have the technology to live there should we wish. And so humanity is entering upon a new exploration, a new adventure—to explore ourselves, seeking out new realities, new ways of consciously perceiving the world, new cognitive maps, new ways of being here, new ways of becoming more and more "human", more and more aware whole men and women.

THE ROAD TO ELSEWHERE—ANOTHER DEVELOPMENT

A CALL FOR A NEW PATH

We now come to the core of this presentation. If we reject the mechanistic model of development, then where do we go from here? For ideas or theories or perceptions, as daring or attractive as they may be, are just that unless they lead to concrete policy directions and action. A radical shift in perceptions, policy orientation, and action programs is obviously required.

Without difficulty, I join my voice with those of other international commentators who see mankind at a crossroads, with those who call for a program for human survival. I view the current world situation that seriously too. I also agree with those who see the current economic difficulties in the industrialized nations, which of course flow into the developing nations as spin-offs, not as just another world recession or depression but as an event that is much more dangerous.

Furthermore, my assessment is yet more harsh, so that I join persons like James Robertson and Ronald Higgins, both former staff members to British prime ministers, and Hazel Henderson of the United States, who state that what we are seeing are the major symptoms of breakdown and collapse of the Western economic system as now structured. I will go beyond that and state that the current social order of the West, the foundation which supports that economic system, is even further on the road to collapse.

Our constructed reality now totters. In this sense—and the data are there to be seen—the Western approach to reality, and therefore to the economy, and therefore to its other social institutions including the family, is coming apart. If there are no radical changes in these approaches in the coming, immediate years, we will all be living with, and affected by, a worldwide failure.

Some might say that this is sheer pessimism. I say that it is simply realism. When a doctor tells us that a patient needs intensive hospital care, we do not call him a pessimist and walk out. No! We accept the diagnosis and set out to do what we can. There are too many creditable world leaders, from Kurt Waldheim, Secretary-General of the United Nations, on down, who tell us, day in and day out, that we who inhabit this planet are now living on a knife edge.

As noted earlier, the most crucial historical stage of Western development, and the point where the rot sets in from the beginning, was and remains our blatant destruction of community. Through our kind of evolving institutional structures we fostered the increasing attenuation of close, human interrelationships, whether experienced in the family, in the neighborhood, in the work place, or in the countryside. Whether through rank individualism in those Western countries that follow one form or another of a modified free enterprise system, or whether through socialist structures that seek to create an artificial form of community that equally attenuates basic human relationships, we of the West have blindly sought to exploit the planet materially. Both of these variations on the common Western theme are, by their very nature, feeding and accelerating the generalizing breakdown that is already well under way.

THE WESTERN WAY OF LIFE: A CORE PLANETARY ISSUE

Yes, the Western way of life still shows much glitter and glamor, as can be seen in Hong Kong. But let us remember it could be all snuffed out very quickly. In a nuclear holocaust, it could be gone in minutes. In a less disastrous situation, the breakdown of the international banking and monetary system could turn down the lights and finish the twinkle in a couple of days. Hence, the Western way of life and its supporting institutional structures are in dire need of reconstruction and of redevelopment.

I also agree with the many commentators that the great social and economic issue is still poverty on the planet. But the answer is not more but fewer Western-style financial institutional approaches, presently straining and groping to find new ways to enable the poorer nations to borrow more, on even easier terms, when they are already so inundated and incapacitated by the debt service payments, let alone the debts themselves. There is just no room to weave about any more. The problem is not how the poor will find money; the problem is how the rich will give it up.

Even more deeply, the fundamental issue is not how the well-off nations will give up their weatlth, it is how they will shift their way of life, a way of life that seeks constant material growth, where individualism fosters human greed, where the institutionalized fragmentation of people and their relationships creates enormous and costly dependency and alienation. The initial policy stance on the road to the redevelopment of the industrialized nations has to come to terms with this basic present life-style issue.

When the latest, highly commendable and most humanly concerned, international report, that of the Brandt Commission, following upon and repeating the recommendations of the Pearson Commission two decades ago, calls for the wealthier nations to turn over 0.07 percent of their GNP to international aid by 1985, and to bring it up to one percent by the turn of the century, our Western madness becomes all too obvious. Rather, what the industrialized nations and, more important, their peoples, face is a reduction in their standard of living in the order of 30 percent, 40 percent, perhaps 50 percent, over the next decade or two. And to be clear, I am also one of those who suggests that if steps are not taken in this direction voluntarily, the sheer weight of now accumulating international circumstances will take us that far or perhaps further, with or without any help.

To emphasize my point, Western economies, and their money systems, are now being held in thralldom by the OPEC cartel, and I note this without judgment. In one sense, it may be one of the better, though painful, things that has happened to us, for it is forcing us to look at ourselves and how we live.

Let me also remind you that while petro-energy is a major point of international stress, it is not the only one. It emphasizes the mythological character of the current economic order. The OPEC nations, now garnering hundreds of billions of American and Eurodollars into their treasuries, are at this point having trouble in circulating and reinvesting these enormous, high-impact paper earnings. But we all know that if the various interdependent industrial money systems come apart under the strains, this wealth that they have gathered will quickly become worth nothing more than the paper on which it is both written and printed. In the energy game, the danger is symbiotic and moving well in the direction of a zero-sum game, that is, a situation where there are no winners and all are losers.

What the industrialized nations have attained, without exception, is important. First, everyone every day eats enough, or more than enough at the least to sustain life, and often, at the best, to foster growth. This is a gigantic social and economic breakthrough. Second, they have attained high technological capacities. Frequently to be found is a relative measure of political freedom. These are all great strengths.

While these are historical, human breakthroughs of a very high order seen across the millenniums of history, and while these gains in principle need to be maintained if we are all to survive on this planet, Western people have no choice but to seek their continuance in a radically new fashion and to prepare for major life modifications. To wit, the present capacity to eat enough in some countries requires that it no longer be done at the expense of others—at the price of relative or severe hunger for half the population of the planet, for two billion of our fellows, who go to bed hungry each night or who die of starvation. Their bare food lockers and shelves stand as stark witness to the mounds of edible garbage now inundating industrial countries.

Moreover, our technologies are mindless. They radiate and multiply without moral constraint or regard for their social and psychological impact on people. Reflect only, for instance, upon the as yet little seen but very advanced and possibly cancerous growth of robotics through microprocessors in industry, commerce, and warfare systems. Today they contribute severely to the redundancy of workers, of people. They could contribute to human well-being but not under the current rubrics of introduction and application.

This new technological, economic, and social innovation does provide us with an impetus, a motivation, and an urgent need to reshape our way of life. While the effects of the microprocessor could be disastrous, it could ease the burden of labor for all. As such, it provides us with an opportunity to shape a new way of life in keeping with the needs of our fellows throughout the planet.

Production is becoming independent of a mass labor force. In the same fashion that the pill has broken the connection between sexual activity and child rearing, similarly the microprocessor is a major contributor to severing the link between work and income.

Hence we are no longer faced with the simple issue of how we can improve our current social security programs for those citizens in our industrialized societies whose incomes from personal or family earnings are nil or minimal. Nor are we looking at a review and expansion of our normal manpower training and retraining programs to mop up the current relatively small numbers of our unemployed. Rather, those of us involved in these fields of social welfare are being called upon to rethink our overall national income-distribution systems, to rethink the meanings of our concepts of work itself, and to design transition and follow-through programs and opportunities whereby people's own capacities, talents, and imaginations are liberated and set into motion, so that new modes of human working activity, paid and unpaid, become valued and recognized, become legitimated, furthered, and fostered within our societies. Here begin the paths to a new life style.

ANOTHER MODE OF DEVELOPMENT

Despite the systemic problems, we can continue to intensify our present efforts to realize our own personal humanity and that of others, whether at home, at work, at play, or at prayer. We can become more aware and direct our efforts toward those many others in our home cities and in our homelands with and for whom we all work and carry out our daily tasks. We can try to learn more about ourselves and try to put into effect within our jobs the criterion that people, not systems, come first. As life has schooled us differently to live and work within bureaucratic system models, it is no easy task to understand and implement this simple human criterion in our everyday working lives. Thus, for a change, our first change target is ourselves, not others. Moreover, it begins in our minds, in our perceptions, and not in our budgets and programs.

Another mode of development requires another understanding and another kind of implementation. Development as such is not and cannot be a goal. It is a resultant and outcome of a wide variety of other activities, which once realized and taken together constitute a state of human development, or said better still, constitute a context of developing. It ' egins with ourselves, then and only then with others.

In light of what I have said, no longer can we say that Western nations are developed and others, because they are poorer, are not. The West needs development, its own kind of *re*development, as badly as the hungrier nations on this earth need their own kind of development. And so we talk as equals, all of us badly in need of help to develop better and to build up or restore our human capacities and response. In all cases it will require of each of us all we have to give in reflection, in growing understanding, in caring, in collaborating, in realizing the strengths and potential in all of us and in all our peoples.

ANOTHER DEVELOPMENT FOR THE INDUSTRIALIZED NATIONS

Of the differing modes of developing that are called for, the style for those from the so-called economically developed nations is specific to them. While most difficult to implement, the basic policy guidelines that can be suggested for the industrialized nations are relatively simple. They are not based on a simplistic approach of transferring either one percent or 40 percent of the GNP from the wealthy nations to the poorer, though this would in effect eventuate itself at some fairly high rate of magnitude in a new international economic order. Rather, my suggested directions for new approaches and programs are aimed at modifying the generic mindset and life-style pattern that permeate the way of life found in the industrialized nations.

The keys to the road for developing the Western, the industrialized nations, are threefold:

1. The fostering of a new simplicity in life style directed to improving its quality
2. A return to community and the furtherance of human interrelationships
3. The nurturance of relative, self-sufficient interreliance among familial groups, neighbors, communities, regions, and nations.

Simplicity, community and self-sufficient interreliance. Simplicity means essentially learning to relax and live a little. Though the rat-race way of life is winding down, who really wants its pressures? It means learning to live again more easily with self and others, cooperating more, doing more for ourselves. It means conserving and improving our homes, equipment, and communities. It means turning away from waste and obsolescence, and turning to greater durability and longevity in our goods, appliances, and equipment. It means turning to healthier, life-invigorating life styles. To seek quality rather than quantity does not require putting on a hair shirt. Rather it can be a road to growth, to more satisfying, better contented lives.

To quote my late good friend E. F. (Fritz) Schumacher, author of *Small Is Beautiful,* we need an economics based on "enough" not "more." No longer can Westerners live high on the hog and think that others, far away, are unaware. Nor is it a simple matter of world social justice, which is in fact one aspect of it. Equally important is that the Western barriers be pulled down. We will do it ourselves or have it done to us. Perhaps even more important, our nations and our peoples are growing sick, becoming less human, on the glut of our production, whether for useful or trivial purposes. The time for radical social and economic change, based in people, has arrived.

Such an economics—more important, such a way of life—is based in people and their capacities, not things. The main characteristics of the projects, rooted in the daily life of people, in such an approach are that they be:

1. Culturally defined, locally and regionally
2. Self-administered with collaboration and facilitation from outside as needed
3. Self-scheduled (family and/or community scheduled)
4. People (labor)-intensive
5. Indigenous skill-intensive
6. Small capital-intensive
7. Cooperation-intensive
8. Primary relationship-intensive
9. Self, familial, and/or tribal and community reliance-intensive.

We could thus redefine the economy as having five labor sectors, not the traditional three, to wit:
1. The primary national resource sector
2. The secondary manufacturing sector
3. The tertiary service sector
4. The community mediating (cash and noncash) sector
5. The noncash, familial, home, domestic sector.

Simply stated, we need a new view which encompasses people, their capacities, and contributions wholeheartedly. Rather than destroying community and our basic relationships, we can learn to rebuild upon them. They have always been the core of human development. They remain so. Rather than being ignored or excluded from our economic and societal considerations, they can become central to it. In this way might we do away with the current artificial separations between social and economic programs and policy.

ANOTHER DEVELOPMENT FOR THE LESS INDUSTRIALIZED NATIONS

That I should use the phrase "less industrialized" is in no way a putdown. Rather, the less industrialized a nation is, the easier it will be for it to reset directions in an alternate human fashion in order to further the development, but a form of economic development this time enclosed within, and founded upon, the rubrics of human interrelationships.

One of the characteristics, found equally today in societies with lesser industrial development, is the relative strength of familial, tribal, village, and neighborhood life. It will be less attenuated than it is in the industrialized nations. Hence, the challenge before those of us who work in these lands is not to introduce Westernized programs and methods that directly and indirectly attack these fundamental human relationships, but rather to foster those programs and innovate new ones that build on the strength of the family, the tribe, the village, the neighborhood, and the region.

Development does not have to be found mainly in big projects that, as an afterthought, are said to have good spin-off effects for people. That is our Western style. Rather, development first comes through people, mainly through small, people-sized projects. Their accumulating potential and capacity lead naturally to those large projects that may be needed, though fewer are ultimately needed than we have been led to expect.

As other reports on the international level propose increasingly, the methods and techniques within the new field of intermediate technology (major technology adapted to local, people-size technology rather than mass and large-scale technology applications) provide a new viable way to introduce improved material conditions, more human working conditions, small-scale yet high-level technology production, more integrated human patterns of work and development within people's everyday lives in the smaller communities where they live.

Of course, there will still be need for technology transfers and for money transfers, of a major order compared with what is occurring today, from the industrialized nations to those who have less. But the mode of their local use need not be Western. The main point I make is that in regard to developing programs aimed toward a new kind of development in these countries, I am not proposing some kind of human relationship, utopian love-in feast as the new road to development. Rather, I am proposing a hard-nosed examination of developing social services and other economic and social programs that further basic human relationships, while at the same time introducing an expanding, people-adapted technology. In this fashion, as we further their capacity to eat every day, we also develop their capacities to grow and live better human lives.

The challenge to the developing nations is: can they do an end run around our Western industrial path in creating and expanding their production capacity? Industry, producing sane, useful, and durable products and services, is needed everywhere to improve human life and growth. But do all nations have to use Western style, mass-scale, people-reducing methods and techniques? Cannot industry, human and community industry and industriousness, be led and developed along better, more human paths? In this regard we do have experience. Some is to be found in the Ghandian village movement in India, in China and many of its communes; in Tanzania and its local developmental approaches founded in Ujamaa, a concept that is based in people, familial, and community cooperation. Yes we do have experience, though it is not held in the highest regard. The time has come when we need to go back to it, foster it, learn better from it, and develop as nations in new ways.

WHENCE THE SOCIAL SERVICES?

For the social services, the implications in the shift are equally radical. There are questions, new yet old, that we must once again ask. They are hard ones, different ones. For instance, why are we in the West a people who:

Have little respect for age, for the wisdom of long life experience?
Separate out the elderly and seek to cushion them with panaceas?
Downplay life commitment one for another?
Place children of broken homes with strangers, however kind?
Shut so many women away, with little function, in suburban boxes?
Use strangers so extensively, however well-trained, to bare our souls?
Judge paid work to be the only good and useful work?
Have led men to place jobs constantly before family needs?

Set up a life of nominal or no responsibilities for our young?
Have created a category of "youth," people with no real place in our societies?
Pretend that the only real learning goes on at school, when it is founded in life experience everywhere?

In our emphasis on material reality, as these questions suggest, we have transferred many of our human values to self-centered, money, and material values. We have translated "how we serve one another" into "services," into objects that can be manipulated and paid for, rather than letting them be serving acts freely given. And so, having invaded human activity so deeply and having monetized economic and social activity so extensively, we are now caught in a service society which has become too expensive financially to afford and too costly in terms of alienation and in the extensive breakdown of relationships to long endure. This is why service dependency, creating social assistance and social service programs, can never go anywhere but to a human dead end. This is equally true for the fields of organized health, education, and leisure.

The direction we need today is not the further monetization of close, neighborly, and community activity. The time to demonetize much of our human activity has arrived. Its aready growing dynamic within industrialized nations is apparent in our increasing awareness of, and the actual growth of, what is called nonmonetary informal economic activity, which is deeply human and social in character.

A TIME TO REUNDERSTAND HUMAN WELL-BEING

The social services and their workers—in other words, us—in our desire to help people who have been suffering from crucial social, community, familial, and other relationship breakdowns, have been equally caught in the web of industrialized modes of service. Just as all the institutional structures of the medical and health services in the industrialized nations have become caught up in the concepts of sickness and pathology, having lost sight of health itself in their approaches, so have we in the social fields become confused about the meanings of well-being. Well-being is centered in healthy relationships with others. In other words, we need to learn what patterns lead to healthy relationships, and no longer place our emphasis on the treatment of the pathological aspects once trouble has happened. We need to learn to work with the socially well, to facilitate them to handle their own growth and development. No longer can we continue unconsciously to nourish the excessive dependencies that we and our fellow citizens now suffer under the Western way of life and under our current industrialized social service systems.

The essential approach required will be an act of faith in the capacity of people to help themselves. Translated into programs, it means an increasing and major shift in the direction of supportive work in strengthening and fostering self-help and mutual-aid groups of all kinds, including those in therapeutic situations, throughout our communities.

It will mean encouraging people to expand their familial networks, to develop them where they can with kin, friends, and neighbors, so that all of us once again can live out our lives with the caring support of known committed others about us, whether these are found in conventional marriages or not. The basic issue facing familial life today is not whether one is living with others with or without the sanction of law or religion. Rather, the core issue is the commitment of persons, one to another, one to others. Without commitment, there can be no stable or solid human relationship that can carry those involved through the stresses and pressures of life, particularly under the extreme pressures of societal transition that we are now all going through. Relationship without commitment provides but momentary comfort in the good times, but becomes an empty shell when it is most needed.

Hence the major task of social service workers, whatever their fields, will be to enable people—people working together, ordinary people in their ordinary yet valuable capacities—to support, to help, to be helped, and to be with one another. In other words, all of our efforts have to be redirected toward strengthening "community" within us and among us, whether at the familial, group, neighborhood, or community level. This is so whether it be in the countryside, in the small towns, in the villages, or in the city neighborhoods. There is no other route to go.

The ICSW itself has entered a new sound path. In the regionalization of its structures, it has taken a fundamental step inasmuch as the unconscious heavy North American and European influence is reduced, and the door is opened to local and regional input, experience, and approaches, favoring development fitting to each area.

THE ANSWERS LIE IN THE HERE AND NOW

My main message is simply that *people in community are the way to any development.* Though the problems before us on this planet are horrendous, there is hope. Our hope lies in people, starting with ourselvles.

The answer is not to juggle and jiggle programs and budgets due to the present economic uncertainties. Rather, we can use the times for a new start to enter on another path to development, one vested in people, their needs and their capacities. In essence, the time is arriving to let our program directions arise from the people and hence on to policy. In this fashion the validity of our work can flow from the experience and life of people. Getting close to people is the name of the game for us all.

We all know that great obstacles beset us: rigid policy from above, rigid bureaucracies within which we find ourselves, thinking based in a secure yesterday that is now gone. But each one of us, despite frustrations, can reflect on our earlier aspirations, on our small but solid achievements over the years, and drawing on these, face the challenge now looming.

Hong Kong is a microcosm that says it all. Beneath the modern glitter of this multiracial human enclave are people who know how to endure, how to be resilient, how to be caring, how to succeed in the face of terrible odds. They are us, and we can inspire one another.

Social Welfare Development in Hong Kong in the 1970s

HAROLD HO

CHAIRMAN, CONFERENCE PROGRAM COMMITTEE

FROM THE years immediately following World War II to the early 1970s, the provision of welfare services in Hong Kong was mainly in the form of relief in kind, the mainstay of the welfare sector in the early years being voluntary organizations, including the local traditional ones like the Tung Wah Group of Hospitals and Po Leung Kuk, and others affiliated with religious bodies which brought in substantial support from foreign countries.

The pioneering role in developing welfare services has been the undertaking of the voluntary agencies. The Hong Kong Government, on the other hand, remained in the background up to the 1960s, giving guidance and support to the voluntary sector through the Secretariat for Chinese Affairs at first, and later, through the Social Welfare Department which had developed from a small section in the same secretariat into the present department.

The main concern of the government has always been to maintain a stable environment for economic development, with minimum government intervention unless and until order and stability are threatened. It intervenes effectively, in providing for relief, housing, education, medical, health, or other social services whenever emergency situations demand. Over the years, the eagerness of some policy-makers to push ahead with social development has been dampened by a genuine worry that attractive welfare provisions would bring in too many unproductive and unwanted people from neighboring countries.

Between 1945 and the end of 1950 the population had grown to an estimated 2,360,000 from a mere 600,000 because of an influx of immigrants and refugees during the civil war in China. The feeling then, however, was that the refugees would soon return to their homes in China, once peace and stability were restored there.

The Korean War resulted in a general blockade of China in the early 1950s, leaving a large number of the Chinese refugees stranded in Hong Kong, their plight highlighted in 1952–53 after a huge squatter hut area fire in Shek Kip Mai in Kowloon. The government won wide acclaim by responding with massive emergency resettlement schemes which were the forerunners of impressive housing schemes in years to come.

In May 1965, the Legislative Council adopted a White Paper on Aims and Policy which affirmed that "Hong Kong should continue to make provision for minimum public assistance consisting of shelter, clothing and food, i.e., providing for those of the population who are demonstrably unable to fend for themselves."[1] More sophisticated social welfare services had been envisaged as early as the 1940s, but the continued rapid rise in population had caused them to be postponed indefinitely.[2]

Immediately after publication of the 1965 White Paper, the Social Welfare Department and the Hong Kong Council of Social Service set up a joint planning committee with the "twofold purpose of achieving a 5-Year Plan of development for social welfare services in line with the stated aims and policy whilst at the same time providing a more definitive statement of those aims in relation to such a 5-year period."[3]

This first attempt at the formulation of a five-year plan for

[1] "Aims and Policy for Social Welfare in Hong Kong," a White Paper published by the Hong Kong Government in May 1965, paragraph 9(a).
[2] "Social Welfare in Hong Kong: the Way Ahead," Hong Kong Government (1973), p. 8, paragraph 4.1.
[3] See "An Appreciation of Social Welfare Services and Need in Hong Kong, 1969," produced jointly by the Social Welfare Department and the Hong Kong Council of Social Service, which took the place of the intended 5-Year Plan.

social welfare in Hong Kong did not succeed[4] because plans became out of date while being drawn up. The entrepôt trade of Hong Kong stifled by the Korean War embargo on China had long been replaced by industrialization which had made Hong Kong more prosperous than before. Gaps widened between the rich and the poor.

Disturbances which broke out in 1967 also interfered with any attempts at long-term planning, but once order was restored, experience pointed to the need for more urgent attention to the fact that a new generation had grown up in Hong Kong from the group of so-called refugees who had taken up permanent residence, mostly in unsatisfactory and crowded places originally meant for temporary resettlement only. The time was ripe for a breakthrough that was to come in the 1970s.

DEVELOPMENT IN THE 1970S

In the 1960s, relief in the form of dry rations and cooked meals was provided by the government while, in the main, the voluntary sector rendered counseling and financial assistance. By 1971, the government had taken over full responsibility for public assistance by introducing a cash system of assistance. It had to be somewhat primitive to begin with, but the new scheme marked a breakthrough from the concept inherent in the former type of material relief, given as a charity, in which the recipients had no choice. The cash assistance was an expression of the authority's trust in the ability of the people to buy what was essential for their own subsistence.

In 1973, the government adopted a new White Paper entitled "Social Welfare in Hong Kong: the Way Ahead" and began implementation of the first Five-Year Plan complementing the White Paper, covering the first period from April 1973 to March 1978. The White Paper and the Five-Year Plan were regarded as a model of partnership between the public and

---

[4] The plan did not materialize until the first Five-Year Plan was adopted in 1973.

the private sectors because before their adoption a draft white paper described as a "green paper" had been published to seek the widest possible reactions from voluntary agencies and other groups in the general public.[5]

An unprecedented economic boom in the early 1970s enabled the government to proceed with the Five-Year Plan, which was reviewed each year to keep it rolling on as a Five-Year Plan. With economic considerations foremost in all planning, however, it was not without foresight that the government made it clear that the inclusion of any particular project or activity in the Five-Year Plan would not of itself convey any guarantee of implementation. The reason given was that there could be unforeseeable changes of circumstances and further policy or financial approval might be required.

By April 1973, the public assistance scheme had been extended from the initial means-tested cash assistance for the destitute to other nonmeans-tested allowances to the aged and the severely disabled.[6] Victims and dependents of those killed or injured in violent crimes also began to receive compensation from the government to tide over their immediate financial needs. By May 1979, victims of traffic accidents, regardless of the party to blame, also started to receive prompt assistance in cash.[7]

The pressing needs of the 1970s for preschool child care services resulted in the adoption of the Child Care Centers Ordinance and Regulations in 1976, the outcome of standard-setting by the joint efforts between the voluntary agencies and the government. Since the implementation of the Five-Year Plan, the government has come to the forefront and taken a

[5] A series of "green papers" covering education, medical services, and other major areas was published in the early 1970s soon after the present governor, Sir Murray MacLehose, assumed office, and these continued to be published from time to time, preceding White Papers to be adopted. It has been demonstrated that public opinion did result in improvements or changes to certain aspects of recommendations that appeared in the White Papers.

[6] See T. R. Heppell, "Social Security and Social Welfare: A 'New Look' from Hong Kong," *Journal of Social Policy* (April 1974), 3(2): 113–26.

[7] Introduced in May 1979 to bridge gaps in third-party motor insurance, and the time usually taken for recovery of compensation by legal means which could be a real hardship to traffic accident victims and their dependents.

more positive outlook than before in the provision of welfare services.

A quick comparison of the government expenditure on social welfare between the early 1970s and the latest budget allocation shows that there has been a remarkable development, even allowing for inflation. The commitment of public funds to social welfare in Hong Kong has increased almost four and a half times in the last seven years, from an annual expenditure of about $136.9 million, including subventions to voluntary agencies in 1973–74, the first year of the Five-Year Plan, to $750.5 million in the budget estimates for 1980–81.[8] The largest share has been taken up by social security provisions.

The most significant change in the official stand relating to social development came during the term of office of the present governor, Sir Murray MacLehose. Instead of viewing social services as dependent upon economic growth, the government now attributes greater importance to social development. As Sir Murray put it in his address to the Legislative Council in October, 1976, on the subject of community building: "Our aim must be to build a society . . . in which there is mutual care and responsibility. Our social programs are of course relevant because people will not care for a society which does not care for them."[9]

In the meantime, more green papers similar to that published prior to the adoption of the 1973 White Paper were drawn up between 1976 and 1977, covering services for those least able to help themselves, namely, children and youth, the elderly and the disabled.[10]

The 1979 White Paper, "Social Welfare into the 1980s," in-

---

[8] The 1973–74 and 1980–81 budgets, under "Actual and Estimated Expenditure" for the respective periods including actual expenditure for the immediately preceding periods.

[9] See address at the opening session of the Legislative Council on October 6, 1976, p. 13.

[10] A series of four green papers was produced by the government during the period, laying down the intention of the government in regard to the development of the various social welfare services: "The Further Development of Rehabilitation Services in Hong Kong," October 1976; "Help for Those Least Able to Help Themselves," November 1977; "Development of Personal Social Work among Young People in Hong Kong," November 1977; and "Services for the Elderly," November 1977.

corporated most of the recommendations in the green papers published earlier, and has been regarded by the professional community as a document updating the 1973 White Paper.

Besides expansions in the social security system, the government has also extended facilities for community development, improved the quality and scope of family welfare services and services for the disabled and the elderly, along with statutory facilities for probation and correctional services.

With the government assuming full responsibility for public assistance at the turn of the decade, the voluntary agencies were enabled to make substantial progress in new ventures besides expanding existing services and raising standards of service. In family service, the most rapid development was in child care, with an increase in the number of child care centers from only fifty in 1970 to more than two hundred toward the end of the decade, and the standards of such centers were regulated by law following adoption of the Child Care Centers Ordinance and Regulations in 1976. New ventures in family service included home help service, school social work, and family life education.

In youth work, besides rapid expansion in the number of youth centers, camps, and hostels, and the number of activities of a recreational nature, the voluntary sector also made great strides in developing outreaching social work which is now being undertaken by eight voluntary agencies in sixteen different districts, providing counseling services and detached social work to meet the needs of youths in the districts.

With varying degree of support from the government, the voluntary agencies were able to initiate, promote, and develop facilities and services in community development and rehabilitation and to expand the scope of services for the elderly which, prior to the 1970s, used to be mainly in the form of residential homes run by religious and charitable bodies.

The prosperity of Hong Kong in the 1970s resulted in a sharp reduction of overseas funding, on which many voluntary agencies depended for the provision of welfare services. Much of the funding had been channeled to meet more pressing needs of other countries in the region. The inevitable outcome has been an increasing dependence of the voluntary sector on public funds for service delivery and expansion projects.

Finance was not the only major problem confronting voluntary welfare agencies. The problem of manpower shortage was just as serious. The need for trained social workers has been felt since the 1960s. Although some steps were taken to alleviate the shortage, the demand still exceeds the supply, and the situation has been aggravated by a high turnover of social welfare personnel of about 14.8 percent in 1979,[11] and about 8 percent in wastage of trained students who joined other fields.[12]

CHALLENGES AHEAD IN THE 1980S

The 1979 White Paper has incorporated expansions in the social security system, but has not yet covered basic protection against sudden loss of income such as a sickness, injury, and death benefit scheme mentioned in one of the green papers preceding the White Paper, not to mention provision against the more gradual loss of earning capacity from old age. The sudden and large-scale inflow, once more, of Chinese immigrants following a change in the political climate in the 1970s and the problem of Vietnamese refugees has intensified the pressure of the greatly enlarged population, now estimated at more than 5.5 million, and has necessitated a total revision of many of the development plans previously made or suggested.

On the other hand, the aspirations of the populace, particularly those who have grown up in Hong Kong and have contributed toward its economic prosperity, cannot be met by the prospect of mere subsistence when they retire. Meeting the expectations of the people with adequate welfare provisions without threatening the economic foundation of Hong Kong will be the greatest challenge to policy-makers. There will also

---

[11] "Report on the Social Welfare Manpower Survey 1980," prepared by a joint working group of the Social Welfare Department, Hong Kong Government, and the Hong Kong Council of Social Service, published in June 1980, paragraph 6.4.
[12] *Ibid.,* paragraph 6.6.

be a need to maximize the effectiveness of resources invested in such provisions, and the equally important need to have a balance in maintaining the attractive environment for overall growth of Hong Kong.

The development of social welfare in Hong Kong in the 1970s has been a marked achievement in spite of rapidly changing circumstances, not always favorable, during the decade. As Hong Kong steps into the 1980s, greater challenges presented by the accelerated pace in population growth through immigration should not prove to be any more difficult than challenges of the 1970s, because there is now a more positive outlook in social development.

The Hong Kong Government has already assumed a leading role in providing basic and essential welfare services, and in channeling the energies and resources of the private sector by means of subventions and policy directives to attain the planned goals. The voluntary sector has also shown its willingness and support in its pioneering and consultative roles based on mutually agreed aims and objects.

In the final analysis, the 1980s will usher in a sense of belief and commitment in the future well-being of Hong Kong through improving relationships with China and through Hong Kong's contribution to its modernization programs. With this prospect in mind, social welfare development could enter into a dynamic phase in its evolution.

Refugees in Southeast Asia

HARI BRISSIMI
CHIEF, COUNSELING, EDUCATION, AND RESETTLEMENT SECTION, OFFICE OF THE UNITED NATIONS HIGH COMMISSIONER FOR REFUGEES

THE REFUGEE problem viewed in its global entity is unfortunately not subsiding. It is, in fact, escalating and is a reflection of the deteriorating world situation; it has, indeed, become one of the most pressing humanitarian problems of our times. It is therefore most appropriate that the ICSW should focus attention on it, particularly since Southeast Asia is an area in which the repercussions of the refugee problem are deeply felt.

Before turning to the situation of refugees in Southeast Asia, however, let me outline briefly the refugee problem all over the world as it stands today, to permit us to focus our attention on a particular theme within the context of the global picture.

Because of a well-founded fear of persecution for reasons of race, religion, nationality, political opinion, or membership in a particular social group, more and more people leave their homes and sometimes their families, flee their country of origin (or habitual residence) and seek asylum in another. Once outside their own country and unwilling to avail themselves of its protection, they are considered refugees. The refugees' expectation in fleeing is to live free from such fear. Those whom the Office of the United Nations High Commissioner for Refugees (UNHCR) is helping today are to be found in many continents. In addition to the refugees, persons displaced as a result of man-made disasters are also receiving assistance from UNHCR as the High Commissioner has been empowered by the relevant Economic and Social Council and General Assembly resolutions to deal also with such persons.

In Africa the main concentrations of refugees are in Somalia, in the Sudan, in Cameroon, in Angola, in Mozambique, in Zaire; in fact, in more than twenty countries there are almost 4 million persons of concern to UNHCR.

In Latin America there are approximately 100,000 refugees of Latin American and European origin, most of whom are by now settled. Recently some 100,000 Nicaraguans repatriated voluntarily to their country.

In Asia there are over 2 million refugees, of whom about 1.2 million arrived in Southeast Asia from the Indochina peninsula and close to 900,000 crossed from Afghanistan into Pakistan.

In Europe, North America, and Oceania there are over 1.8 million, very few of whom are considered as requiring assistance from other than national sources in the country of their asylum.

The funds which UNHCR needs in order to provide the assistance required by refugees in some sixty countries during 1980 to secure care, maintenance, interim services, and durable solutions will most likely reach half a billion dollars, a quite unprecedented level. In 1956, when our program of material assistance to refugees was one year old, $4.5 million were spent. The escalation of needs is eloquently demonstrated through these two figures.

In addition to these contributions, governments of countries of first asylum or resettlement, other intergovernmental organizations, and many voluntary agencies dispose of funds, time, energy, ideas, and commitment and join forces with UNHCR in trying to meet the basic human needs of refugees and provide the services they require. The task is not easy because of the constraints within which we must often operate. Such constraints can produce the type of problem which those coming into contact with the refugees feel should not exist. We might refer, for example, to the preoccupation with national security on which countries of asylum have at times placed particular emphasis. People who have visited refugees know what this can often entail in practice in a refugee camp.

To harmonize concerns of this kind (and the constraints deriving from them) with the concern for meeting the basic human needs of refugees as effectively and humanely as possible is not an easy endeavor. This is, in fact, the challenge for UNHCR to insure appropriate service to refugees notwithstanding the differing and at times conflicting concerns. It is befitting for a subsidiary body of the UN General Assembly, UNHCR, whose functions are humanitarian and social, to pursue such a goal. In the process UNHCR has been awarded the Nobel Prize for Peace.

The primary and most urgent humanitarian need of a refugee is obviously to receive asylum. Thus other countries must agree to open their doors to refugees fleeing their own country. This is a matter on which the governments concerned, usually those of countries neighboring the one which the refugees are leaving, may need the help and persuasion of UNHCR in order to comprehend, accept, and incorporate in their policy. UNHCR might have to overcome resistance in that respect despite the fact that in Article 14 of the Universal Declaration of Human Rights it is stated that "everyone has the right to seek and to enjoy in other countries asylum from persecution." To facilitate matters in that connection in terms of relations between states, the United Nations Declaration on Territorial Asylum which confirmed the principle of *nonrefoulement* (nonreturn to the country of origin), stipulated that the grant of asylum by a state cannot be regarded by any other state as an unfriendly act.

Examples of asylum being denied were widely reported in the press last year when boat people were pushed off shores and refugees were sent back to their country of origin across borders—examples of UNHCR endeavors to protect refugees and establish their right to asylum, but which on these occasions were not successful.

The objectives of international protection of refugees are not limited to securing asylum. In the country of asylum such protection should provide for the refugee to be granted legal status as close as possible to that of nationals resident in that country, particularly as regards civil, economic, social, and cultural matters.

As mentioned in the Background Paper on UNHCR prepared for this conference:

> The legal status of refugees has been defined more particularly in two international instruments adopted on the universal level, namely, the United Nations 1951 Convention and the 1967 Protocol relating to the Status of Refugees. These instruments define the rights and duties of refugees and contain provisions dealing with a variety of matters in the day-to-day life of the refugee, e.g., the right to work, public assistance, social security. In regard to many of these matters, refugees are to receive the same treatment as nationals of their country of residence.

Since there is no UNHCR State, it is countries of potential asylum which must be ready both to open their doors to refugees reaching their territory, and to treat them humanely and in accordance with the provisions embodied in the Convention, the Protocol, and other relevant instruments which define the refugees' basic rights or human rights in general. Here again we must deal with another possible constraint—that of public sentiment in the country of asylum. In countries where the standard of living of the local population is low, services to refugees can generate the type of envy that may cause negative reactions and influence public sentiment, in turn coloring the official stand on refugees in that country. In such circumstances, UNHCR must use its ability to interpret refugee needs and insure that the refugees survive, that their health is not impaired, and that their dignity is preserved. There have been situations in which UNHCR had to intervene in order to insure that the necessary nutritive food was provided to refugees and that other basic necessities such as primary health care were available, when those responsible for such care, in their concern over possible local reaction, envisaged limiting assistance to a precarious level. Countries of asylum are thus advised as required of the concern of the international community that the basic rights of refugees should be inviolable.

REFUGEES IN SOUTHEAST ASIA

The refugee problems in Southeast Asia originated from the political changes in Indochina in the spring of 1975. Following these changes an increasing number of people left their countries by land and sea and sought asylum in neighboring ones. The exodus reached dramatic proportions in the spring of 1979, and the monthly arrivals reached the peak of 60,814 in June of that year.

From the spring of 1975 to May 31, 1980, more than 635,000 persons left the Socialist Republic of Vietnam, Laos, and Kampuchea, their countries of origin or habitual residence, and arrived overland or on boats in Thailand, Malaysia, Indonesia, the Philippines, Singapore, Hong Kong, and Macao. A few actually reached Northern Australia in small boats. Those rescued by ships and transferred to them from their own boats were most frequently disembarked in countries in the Southeast Asia region, including Korea and Japan, but at times ended up in distant ports such as Mombasa or Rio de Janeiro. The 635,000 do not include the 130,000 persons evacuated and admitted into the United States in mid-1975, or the Kampuchean influx into Thailand from October 1979 onward, of whom some 165,000 are in holding centers under the care of UNHCR. Over and above these movements, some 150,000 Kampucheans crossed into the Socialist Republic of Vietnam, the vast majority of whom repatriated to Kampuchea in the course of 1979, while those remaining are being assisted to attain self-sufficiency in Vietnam or to resettle. Finally, some 263,000 persons crossed from Vietnam into the People's Republic of China where they are being settled with UNHCR assistance.

We are thus viewing a movement across national borders in the Southeast Asia region of some 1.2 million persons who have become uprooted, thereby constituting a vulnerable group—thus being one of the target groups to which the ICSW conference is addressing itself this year.

Since there has been extensive press coverage about those

who came to be known as "boat people," who constitute 54 percent of the 635,000 arrivals to which we referred, it is not necessary to dwell on the details of their odyssey, but we can comment on some of the main points. The refugees who arrived in the first country of asylum, as a rule a country neighboring the Indochina peninsula, came often in a state of extreme physical exhaustion. Many had experienced looting, raping and even killing by pirates who pillaged their boats; in some cases this happened several times in the course of a journey. One can envisage the psychological effects of such experiences. Recent surveys show that of the 166 boats which reached Thailand in the period March–June 1980, 150 had been attacked a total of 527 times. The figures for boats arriving in Malaysia are similar: of the 106 boats arriving in the period April–June 1980, 49 had been attacked a total of 170 times.

The world was shocked to know of the suffering of those who survived—some of them emaciated and maimed—but will never know the numbers of those who perished in their attempts to find a secure refuge. Their sacrifice has aroused the most compassionate response among the international community.

Those who finally arrived on mainland beaches or deserted islands frequently bore the signs of the trauma they had lived through. With the driving force of reaching a new land gone, signs of diminished mental and physical resistance were evident. Malnutrition, especially among the most vulnerable members of this group, coupled with unpalatable conditions in congested camps, caused serious problems of health and welfare.

As more and more refugees arrived, the reaction of neighboring countries was colored by concern over increasing backlogs, since they did not countenance local settlement of refugees and resettlement outside the region absorbed only a proportion of the arrivals. An increasingly insistent demand for the resettlement in third countries of all these refugees developed while some of the countries which the refugees reached following their escape practiced *refoulement* despite the fact that the refugees could face death in their country of origin or perish in the high seas. Some did indeed drown not far from the shore when their boats capsized after being pushed off. Luckily, a good number of refugees who were drifting—having been left to their own resources by the pirates or having run short of fuel—were rescued by merchant ships. A further complication then arose: some countries in the area established the practice of not allowing the ships to disembark these refugees at their first port of call unless they received firm guarantees for their resettlement in another country. The assurances given by UNHCR that we would cover the care and maintenance costs and use our best endeavors to effect their resettlement did not convince certain countries to change that practice. As a result, the ships had to carry a few Vietnamese refugees to far-off places on other continents.

After their arrival in countries of temporary asylum the refugees had, of course, to be provided with the necessary care while plans for durable solutions could be developed. The three classical durable solutions for refugees all over the world are: voluntary repatriation to the country of origin or habitual residence; local integration in the country of asylum; and resettlement in a third country.

REPATRIATION

When repatriation is voluntary, and provided it is feasible, it contains the elements of a very desirable solution. It helps the refugees maintain their roots and saves them from the problem of preparing for, and adjusting to, a new country possibly different in its socioeconomic-cultural milieu; it also saves the host countries, and others involved, from difficult undertakings and diversion of resources for the benefit of refugees. Furthermore, it usually confirms that the causes giving rise to the problem of refugees no longer persist—a healthy development for international peace. In the Southeast Asia context, very few except the Kampucheans who returned from Vietnam have availed themselves of this solution—some 10 percent of the 1.2 million persons who were uprooted.

LOCAL INTEGRATION

The second alternative, local integration in the country of asylum, is in course in an extensive way in the People's Republic of China where some 265,000, over 20 percent of the refugees displaced in the area, are now being integrated locally, having crossed into China from Vietnam. They are assisted by the government of the People's Republic of China and, where necessary, by UNHCR to settle in rural areas. Efforts to promote local integration schemes in other countries of first asylum in the area have not, however, come to fruition, even though local integration in an area neighboring the refugees' country of origin usually helps minimize the cultural shock and thus would obviously be a most useful solution for refugees who seek a new home.

RESETTLEMENT

Resettlement to third countries, therefore, became out of necessity the prevalent solution to the problem of refugees from the Indochina peninsula since the countries of first asylum in the region did not consider that they had the capability to absorb the increasing number of refugees and see them settled locally and since voluntary repatriation was not sought. In various communiqués most of these countries, singly or collectively, maintained that refugees arriving from Vietnam, Laos, and Kampuchea would have to be resettled elsewhere. In the face of persistent demand for the resettlement of the refugees outside the region, the international community from the spring of 1975 onward performed a memorable act of international response by admitting progressively larger numbers of refugees. By May 31, 1980, 427,000 refugees had been resettled in some 30 countries, all but 3 percent of them outside the Southeast Asia region. This means that 35 percent of the total number of the 1.2 million uprooted people were provided with resettlement as a durable solution.

When it comes to refugee resettlement, the UNHCR has to insure that it is carried out effectively. It is thus necessary to plan, orchestrate, and oversee each operation in order to in-

sure that gaps and duplications are avoided and that other organizations involved can make their contributions within a well-defined overall plan. The UNHCR role in the Indochina resettlement operation has been:
1. To seek offers of admission from countries of potential resettlement
2. To discuss criteria of admission to insure that a fair chance for resettlement is provided to refugee applicants
3. To document the refugees as required
4. To counsel the refugees about potentialities for resettlement
5. To facilitate the work of the selection missions
6. To finance the parts of the resettlement operation which are not covered through other sources. (UNHCR funding for example has been used for the transportation of the refugees, their documentation, language training, resettlement counseling, resettlement grants, etc.)

In addition to the government services, whose role in refugee resettlement is primordial, organizations playing a part in resettlement operations are: the Intergovernmental Committee for European Migration, which arranges the transportation of Indochinese refugees from countries of asylum to countries of resettlement at the request of countries of admission, or on behalf of UNHCR, and provides required medical examinations and documents needed to meet predeparture requirements; the International Committee of the Red Cross (ICRC), which frequently is asked to provide travel documents; last but not least, a number of voluntary agencies which engage either in preparing the refugees for resettlement when they are in countries of asylum or in helping them with their integration when they arrive in countries of resettlement.

Since 1975 in a series of appeals, UNHCR, and in 1979 the Secretary-General of the United Nations also, urged states members of the United Nations to offer generous quotas for the admission of refugees for resettlement as well as to provide funds to finance the program of assistance. UNHCR consistently kept the governments informed of the needs of the growing number of Indochinese refugees in camps across Southeast Asia, pointing to the build-up of numbers in the camps. The response was appreciable, but not adequate to match the requirements. The rapidly rising influx in the latter part of 1978 and the first part of 1979, reports about the harrowing experiences of the boat people, and action taken by the countries of first asylum to underline the urgency of the situation all indicated that events had reached crisis proportions. The Secretary-General of the United Nations, acceding to the requests of concerned governments, convened in Geneva on July 20-21, 1979, a meeting on refugees and displaced persons in Southeast Asia, attended by sixty-five countries, many represented by their foreign ministers. In urging participating countries to increase their resettlement offers, the head of one delegation stated: "History will not forgive us if we fail. History will not forget us if we succeed."

In fact, in the course of five years the Indochina resettlement operation has seen the average number of monthly departures for resettlement increase more than tenfold from some 2,000 to 25,000. This is equivalent to practically 1,000 refugees leaving Southeast Asia for resettlement elsewhere on each working day at present.

Monthly Departures

1975-76	1977	1978	1979	1980 (5 months)
2,123	1,693	4,291	16,040	24,872
[102][a]	[782]	[2,578]	[11,074]	[14,348]

[a] Figures in brackets represent the boat people components of the total number.

Encouraging as these figures seem, we cannot afford to remain unaware of the darker prospects, already looming large. The resettlement places available at the end of May 1980, were slightly under 125,000, most insufficient to cover the needs of refugees seeking resettlement out of countries of first asylum. As arrivals are taking an upward trend, with concomitant rising demands for resettlement, continued generous offers of admission are urgently required. Participants in this ICSW conference, I hope, can help to enlighten public opinion and the authorities in their respective countries about this grave need.

Countries with announced quotas for resettlement have varying criteria for selection and acceptance. One common criterion is the family reunion of "immediate" family members in the country of resettlement. Other prevalent criteria place emphasis on ties with the receiving country and knowledge of the language of that country. Some countries take a fair cross section of refugees in camps; others look for those who have the potential for becoming self-supporting as rapidly as possible. Fortunately, at least one country admits handicapped refugees by priority, and other countries are willing to accept a number of the less healthy and less qualified. UNHCR efforts are focused on insuring that a durable solution is found for all—"weak" and "strong" alike.

This is where social workers and resettlement counselors in countries of first asylum and in countries of resettlement can play a vital role to insure that handicapped refugees are given a chance to be rehabilitated and settled. UNHCR, through an ongoing promotional effort, aims at insuring prompt acceptance by resettlement countries of the vulnerable members in refugee groups, by seeing to it that such refugees are not forgotten. Positive results have been achieved thus far, as the information received from some countries of first asylum indicates that departures of handicapped cases for countries of resettlement have not fallen behind.

Not only the criteria but also the process of resettlement and the integration of refugees in countries of admission vary from country to country. In some countries the government covers all aspects of such resettlement. In others, voluntary agencies join in partnership with the government in varying degrees in order to assist the refugees in their integration and at times also in the assessment of their potential for such integration before admission.

In the process of integration voluntary agencies are involved in introducing refugees to the community, in familiarizing them with the norms and mores of the new environment and the demands of communication, in helping them utilize their skills to find employment, in placing the children in school, in providing the necessary support until the refugees can attain self-reliance. The process can be long as the refugees strive to make adjustments and adapt to a new way of life, and expertise is required to offset both the frustrations of the refugees and a possible lack of understanding on the part of the community.

It is evident that the integration of refugees in a country of resettlement must be based on a sound plan that takes account of sensitive issues, such as, for example, where the refugees would be placed. If they stay together, it may isolate them from the rest of the community; if they are too dispersed, they may feel lonely and abandoned. In terms of supportive services, if the refugees are left suddenly to fend for themselves without appropriate support, the pressure may prove too much for them to withstand; if they are overprotected, they may develop undue dependence. Provision for in-group and intergroup relations, guided support for adjustments, and adaptation opportunities for self-reliance are some of the most important factors that should receive adequate consideration in preparing the resettlement plan for the refugees' psychosocial and economic integration—and in such matters persons and groups concerned with social welfare can have a lot to say, and expect to be heard.

Since resettlement has been up to now the most prevailing solution to the problem of refugees in Southeast Asia, the refugees' preparation for such resettlement is of critical importance since it not only can facilitate attainment of self-reliance and ease integration upon eventual arrival in the countries of admission, but will also enhance the refugees' eligibility for selection by countries whose criteria encompass skills which can be acquired, such as, for example, language skills.

Efforts at such preparation should aim at providing:
1. Language training to help the refugees communicate in the language of the country of resettlement and become more acceptable for admission

2. Familiarization with the customs and norms in the country of resettlement to facilitate the refugees' adjustment upon arrival
3. Vocational training to promote attainment of self-reliance in the country of admission and enhance eligibility for resettlement
4. Education for children who had to interrupt their schooling and literacy programs for illiterate refugees, thus eliminating difficulties toward their resettlement in certain countries
5. Occupational activities, gainful or otherwise, to prevent apathy or patterns of dependency.

UNHCR has promoted and, wherever necessary, sponsored activities along these lines in camps in collaboration with government services and nongovernmental agencies which are involved in the operation of such programs.

In refugee camps there have been increasing efforts to provide social counselors to help the newly arriving refugees familiarize themselves with the camp management system, enhance their coping capacities, resolve their personal and interpersonal problems; to help them learn about resettlement options; and to focus special attention on the vulnerable groups. These counselors can also assess the degree to which the welfare of the refugees is observed and make appropriate recommendations.

Unaccompanied minors constitute one of the most vulnerable groups among refugees. The term is used to refer to persons under eighteen years of age who at the moment are not in the company of parents or close relatives. They may have become detached from their parents while fleeing or their parents may have died on the way; some left home, usually with their parents' consent, while the parents stayed behind. Comprehensive studies and indicative surveys undertaken in the camps since the latter part of 1979 showed that there were some 5,000 such persons, alone or in sibling groups.

There was great enthusiasm for promoting adoption of these children, especially those under twelve, and UNHCR has been criticized for not facilitating the process of quick adoption. It should be stressed here that the recommendations made by responsible quarters representing umbrella organizations such as the International Council of Voluntary Agencies were against such adoption, in view of the need to continue arrangements for tracing parents or other relatives and to avoid making final decisions on behalf of minors which may require alteration at a later date when such alteration might not be feasible.

Special reference should be made to minors among the Kampuchean group who crossed into Thailand in 1979 about whom press reports abounded and whose condition upon their arrival gave rise to the greatest concern. These children are now under foster care in the camps, either in children's centers cared for by "cottage parents" in family groups of eight or so, or with Kampuchean families in the camps. They receive care, maintenance, schooling, and other necessary services. Each case is under careful study by a team of social workers seconded to UNHCR by Rädda Farnen of Sweden, while tracing parents and relatives is also in course through the circulation of their pictures and biographical data in the various camps where the families might be accommodated. The combined efforts of ICRC and UNHCR are focused on such tracing.

The UNHCR policy relating to resettlement of unaccompanied minors in general stipulates that they would not be placed for adoption, that there would be adequate tracing of families, and that siblings would not be separated. Unaccompanied minors whose family situation has been possible to assess and for whom resettlement has been considered a suitable solution have been resettled in a number of countries.

By the end of May, 1980, Hong Kong had received more than 80,000 boat people. About half of that number had been resettled outside the area as of May 31, 1980. The peak influx was in June 1979, when 22,835 persons arrived in Kong Kong. In fact, Hong Kong, in contrast to Malaysia and Thailand—the other two countries to which the highest number of refugees have arrived—did not receive a massive influx until the spring of 1979. At the end of 1978, for example, when the caseload in Malaysia and Thailand stood at 49,577 and 139,285, respectively, in Hong Kong it was 7,598. It was during 1979 that Hong Kong received the highest number of boat people to arrive in any one country in the area (72,000); in the same year the persons who arrived in Thailand (overland and by boat) reached 77,321, representing the highest influx in the region without counting those who crossed into Thailand from Kampuchea during the last quarter of 1979. During 1980, up to the end of May, 1980, arrivals in Hong Kong have been on a small scale—a total of 2,500; that is, 5 percent of the total of 52,000 arrivals in the area who landed in Hong Kong. Departures from Hong Kong have thus outnumbered arrivals during 1980 by about 6:1. Still, the balance of the 1979 backlog needs to be dealt with since in 1979 arrivals outnumbered departures by 3:1. It is along these lines that UNHCR and countries of resettlement are facing the problem of Indochinese refugees in Hong Kong and monitoring progress in the resettlement operation to offset any disproportionate time lag between arrival and departure in general.

It is hoped that during this conference it will be demonstrated that for all efforts on behalf of refugees to be translated into concrete results to the benefit of refugees, the international community must evidence a high degree of vigilance and sincere commitment to the cause. Enlightened public opinion at the national and international level can help interpret to all concerned the human needs of one of the vulnerable groups of our times—the refugees—whose ranks are swelling at an alarming pace. I am sure that participants in this conference would count themselves among the most vocal proponents of refugee rights, helping to enhance further the international protection of refugees and promote the quality of services they require.

Intercountry Adoption

HANSA APPARAO AND NAJMA M. GORIAWALLA

INDIA COUNCIL OF SOCIAL WELFARE, BOMBAY

THE CONFERENCE workshop on intercountry adoption is a sequel to the special interest seminar held at the Regional Conference of ICSW in Melbourne, Australia, in 1979. This seminar brought into sharp focus the need for a continued dialog between the countries involved in sending and receiving children for adoption. Specifically, this meeting helped to bring out the Asian experience more vividly, and provided a unique opportunity to discuss the issues relating to intercountry adoption, first from the viewpoint of the countries of origin of the children and then from that of the recipient countries.

Among the international forums that have preceded, the most recent one was the United Nations expert group meeting on adoption and foster placement held in Geneva (1978). This meeting was particularly significant since social welfare personnel from the sending countries were invited to participate for the first time, the attendance in earlier seminars and conferences having being limited to those invited from the Western countries only. Efforts were made to obtain pertinent data from the national governments regarding policies, programs, and laws for the protection of children, and wherever possible with special reference to foster care and adoption in the year 1974 through the office of the United Nations Secretary-General. This information was collected by way of a questionnaire. Responses received from sixty-seven governments yielded an account of the "interest and intention of governments to look after unprotected children"[1] and other material of a philo-

---

[1] Background material for the UN expert group meeting of December 1978, prepared by Bette Sprung-Miller, Consultant, International Social Service and International Union of Child Welfare.

sophical nature, but little concerning action plans and programs.

Among the tasks assigned to the 1978 meeting in Geneva were: (1) to prepare a draft declaration of social and legal principles relating to adoption and foster placement of children nationally and internationally; (2) to draft guidelines for the use of governments in the implementation of these principles, as well as suggestions for improving procedures within the context of their social development. The latter aim remained unaccomplished due to the limited time the group had at its disposal.

OBJECTIVE

The workshop brings together representatives of the children's countries of origin and those of the receiving countries to spell out problem areas and to recommend possible corrective measures. This paper serves as a basic document for the workshop. It focuses on the prevailing adoption practices and procedures both in the countries of the children's origin ("sending" countries) and the countries that adopt them ("receiving" countries), in order to identify the major problems and the issues that are repeatedly faced in translating the basic principles of adoption into actual practice. Possible measures are suggested for consideration. It is hoped that identification of the problem areas and suggestions of possible strategies will finally result in the formulation of draft guidelines.

This paper presents:
1. A step-by-step review of the position and procedures followed in the process of intercountry adoptions, in order to illuminate the problem areas
2. A discussion of the legislative and regulatory provisions
3. Elaboration of the role and function of the recommended central adoption resource agency.

Throughout the discussion distinction is made between the "sending" countries and the "receiving" countries. It is assumed that the sending countries are primarily developing countries and the receiving countries in most cases are developed countries. Thus the two categories of countries involved in intercountry adoption are assumed to represent different levels of resources and, consequently, to vary in general service structures. It is, we feel, important to recognize this distinction; for these service structures have a very important bearing on the practices that have evolved as well as on the measures that could be implemented.

THE SENDING COUNTRIES

THE CHILD

The primary responsibility for the child who becomes a subject of intercountry placement rests with the sending country. There is universal agreement that "the best child welfare is good family welfare"[2] and that for a child deprived of his own biological family, permanent substitute care in his own country should be the first alternative to be considered. The government of the country has the responsibility of providing for the basic needs of a child and his family through family welfare programs. However, a realistic consideration of the material resources at the disposal of the governments of many of the developing nations and sociocultural realities suggest that:

1. The major part of the resources employed in family and child welfare services are taken up in the efforts to insure mere physical survival of the children, including those living with their own families.

2. The legitimate claims for the state care and protection of the children deprived of parental or extended family care cannot be adequately fulfilled, due to several resource constraints.

3. Social realities in some of these countries work strongly against the realization of large-scale rehabilitation of children through in-country adoption. The strong cultural attitudes toward out-of-wedlock birth, skin color, certain racial inheritance, bias against caste and class origins, apprehensions about unknown background of the child, and negative physical attributes, handicaps, and age of the child place the children at a great disadvantage for in-country adoption. In such cases in-

[2] Report of the Secretary-General, UN Economic and Social Council E/CN.5/574, January 22, 1979.

tercountry adoptions could be advantageous, provided they are arranged with scrupulously worked-out safeguards and attended by skilled people.

PROCEDURAL STEPS AND PROBLEM AREAS

The existing practices and the problem areas that are more frequently present at each procedural step are reviewed in the following paragraphs:

1. *The process that results in the decision of the child's placement outside the country of birth*

In determining the need for the child's placement in intercountry adoption, several influences combine in a complex way. Individuals, institutions, attitudinal-motivational forces, and political forces exert varying degrees of influence in bringing about the decision.

The single most influential factor could possibly be the high rate of demand for adoptions. The demand in most situations has been the result of by-now familiar reasons of unavailability of children within the developed countries for adoption. Added to this are other factors of relatively recent origin. To some families in developed nations, adoption of children from developing countries has attained a particular meaning. The international network of news media and travel has brought into sharper focus the consequences of the Vietnam War, the continued flow of boat people, and other upheavals and tragedies in that and other regions of the world. Exposure to these tragic events as well as the visible effects of poverty in many developing countries have created a greater awareness and stimulated a much wider interest in their needs, particularly the needs of homeless, deprived children.

Social ethnics that have emerged arouse a sense of personal responsibility for the victims, particularly the children, who become a focal point of attention. It is in the expression of one's commitment toward the reparation of the existing ills that child adoption has acquired tremendous appeal. These developments have contributed, though to some extent unintentionally, to the pressure of demand for children for adoption. There are perhaps not so many children who are homeless and parentless and needing placement as there are parents in other countries who are eager to adopt. At least this possibility provides one of the more convincing explanations for the unbalanced ratio. While there are no reliable statistical data to determine the exact situation, observations in individual developing countries bear out this conjecture.[3]

The specter of numerous children deprived of the basic material needs and amenities of life in the developing countries on the one hand, and eager prospective adoptors on the other, has spurred many individuals and groups to participate in what is seen as a solution of a simple equation of "need" and "want." Thus, along with the increase in the demand there has been a simultaneous increase in the number of organizations and individuals who are drawn into the field of intercountry adoptions. To them the child's intangible and changing needs throughout his process of maturation are much less obvious than his immediate and dramatically visible material needs.

According to a view that has therefore emerged and is shared by a number of people concerned at some level with intercountry adoption, the tremendous material advantages and opportunities gained by the child by being adopted in a developed country make psychosocial, cultural, and personality considerations superfluous. While material advantages themselves cannot insure a better future, crusading zeal for the cause of the deprived child on the part of the prospective parents does not necessarily coincide with the ability to understand and to relate to the individual child's needs. However, the mistaken perceptions prevail and play an important role in the process of assigning a child for placement abroad. Simultaneously, the possibility of his remaining with his own family, or placement in foster care, or adoption within the country remains unexplored; and efforts to promote in-country adoption are underinvested.

Major child-care facilities. Careful consideration of alterna-

[3] "We do not have very many totally abandoned children available for adoption, as was publicized by some private agents. Most of the children in institutions have their parents," Renu Jotidilok, Director-General, Department of Public Welfare, Thailand.

tives obviously requires a network of agencies concerned with family and child welfare and coordinated action on the part of the givers of care. A review of the major childcare facilities in the sending countries is necessary in this context.

Apart from the traditional and customary care within the extended family or the community for an orphaned child, the major form of care provided to the child who becomes an orphan, is deserted, or is otherwise in need of substitute care for a temporary, permanent, or uncertain period of time, is in residential care institutions. Family assistance programs, formal organization of foster care services, and incountry adoption services are by and large nonexistent or negligible. The welfare services designed for general provision in the area of family and child welfare lack the necessary apparatus and qualified personnel to cover the intensive and specialized child welfare service areas.

Residential child care institutions vary widely in a number of characteristics. They range from being a one-man, charitable, private organization to a sectarian or nonsectarian charitable organization funded by a "family trust." They can also be funded by mixed sources or can be entirely financed by the government. The size, composition, and quality of care and the size of the staff also vary. There are also variations in the delegation of authority to those involved in decision-making on behalf of the child.

Institutions are at the present time the key resources providing minimum care to the destitute. They provide one point where the matter of a child's rehabilitation is potentially amenable to study and to social control.

The decision-makers for the child (whether the child is in the custody of an institution, is being coursed through one for the purpose of adoption, or is in temporary guardianship of an individual or an agency) are in many instances not equipped with means of either understanding the implications of transcultural placements or coordinating with other organizations in search of alternatives. Where the profit motive is predominant, alternative considerations are obviously irrelevant. In the present situation, therefore, there is a wide scope for profit-seekers to determine the future of a number of children who become the subjects of intercountry adoptions; and for nonprofit-seekers to err in their judgment regarding the child's need for placement outside his country of birth.

2. *Determination of the real status of the child*

The real status of the child is often obscure. A number of obstacles are encountered in establishing the status of the child. There are few clues available to trace the antecedents of a lost and/or abandoned (by accident or design) child because of several factors:

a) Lack of fixed place of abode for a large number of the urban poor

b) Inadequate machinery to enforce registration of births; apathy or lack of awareness on the part of a sizable population about the birth registry system

c) Children born out of wedlock, who, for obvious reasons, are hardly ever registered.

The difficulties faced in this respect by institutions whether privately run or government operated are compounded by the lack of adequate resources to trace the antecedents of the child. The same situation is faced by the juvenile courts. Furthermore, the influences and pressures brought to bear by the interested parties to get a child as early as possible may prevent completion of proper inquiries and restoration of the child to his rightful parents wherever this is indicated.

3. *Placement*

There are a number of variations in this process. Some countries insist on the completion of preadoptive requirements in the prospective parents' home country. This means that they have been evaluated for their suitability and approved to bring in a foreign child to their home for the purpose of adoption according to the laws of the in-country after a stipulated period of supervision. In such cases, the child is placed on a preadoptive basis either through a court order of guardianship in favor of the would-be parents, or through authorization by an approved adoption authority.

In some other countries, applications are accepted directly from the prospective parents in person. In these cases the need for evaluation of the parents in their own home country is not insisted upon. The so-called evaluation is done on the spot and legal formalities of adoption completed, before the child leaves the country. Here, unless the prospective parents' home country stipulates the conditions of preadoptive approval and supervision before they are allowed to bring in the child, the whole process takes place in the child's country. While it is helpful for the parents to see the child's country and have personal contact with the agency before a child is placed with them, the family cannot be adequately assessed under these conditions since they are being evaluated in an alien environment. Moreover, the interests of the child in such situations are not safeguarded since no agency is involved in postplacement supervision in the parents' own country (the child being legally theirs) which may intervene should some problems of adjustment arise.

In some other countries a combination of these two procedures exists. After completion of preadoptive requirements in the adoptive parents' own country, adoption and/or guardianship takes place in the country of the child's origin by proxy.

4. *Mutual selection of adoptive parents and child*

In this process, consideration is given, at the most, only to the general characteristics of the preferred child. Even this is ignored in some cases. Final evaluation of suitability and matching of mutual needs are virtually absent due to lack of coordinating procedures between sending and receiving countries, and in some instances to lack of competent and concerned staff in charge of decision-making in institutions having custody of the children. This process assumes critical importance, particularly when older children are concerned.

5. *Legitimation of the child's status with respect to the new family*

Numerous variations exist in this process, depending on the statutory provisions and requirements of both the sending and the receiving country. The legal provision for adoption is absent in some sending countries. Where it does exist, there may be an absence of reciprocal recognition of the legal decree in the receiving country. For example, adoption legitimized under a customary law is not recognized by some countries. Deficiencies of this kind may leave the child with an uncertain legal status.

The authority involved in legitimizing the new relationship in the child's country is vested in either the judiciary or the executive authority. This situation also creates some confusion as far as the recognition of validity of the documents are concerned.

6. *Emigration*

Some national governments do not exercise any control over the emigration of its minors, such as restrictions on issuing passports. This situation readily lends itself to trafficking in children.

RECEIVING COUNTRIES

PROSPECTIVE FAMILIES

There is a broad range of variations among background and motivation of the families who seek intercountry adoption. While the adoption of a child of another race and country is definitely a second choice for some, the child symbolizes a cherished ideal of universal humanity to some others. It is in most cases a complex mixture of motivations. Tolerance and understanding of the procedural requirements also vary widely. While a very small minority disregard safeguards totally and seek to circumvent the established procedures, a large majority of adoptive parents choose to comply with the requirements laid down in the respective countries.

1. *Establishing eligibility and suitability*

Eligibility criteria established to qualify for adoption of children vary widely from country to country. The standards applied in determining the suitability also differ, both between countries and from state to state within a country (North America and Australia). Moreover, standards applied in in-country adoption are not necessarily the same for a foreign adoption, when they are often lowered. Furthermore, professional standards of the agencies involved in assessing the prospective parents are not of the same level. In some instances this results in the approval of unsuitable families for intercountry adoption.

2. *Finding a child*

This is the point in the process where maximum exploitation occurs. The primary reason may be found when exclusive responsibility for identifying children does not rest with authorized agencies. This leaves the field open for private, independent negotiations. Money motives easily enter the process. In the absence of recognized and responsible channels, the child's interests become secondary or are thoroughly compromised. "It is this kind of situation, *inter alia*, that has made the Sri Lanka Government consider the continuity of intercountry adoptions."[4] In addition, the authorized agencies of the receiving countries themselves are handicapped in identifying the right contacts in the absence of appropriate and authorized channels in the child's country.

3. *Selection of adoptive parents*

In a majority of the countries, prospective parents are approved without specifying the characteristics of the child for whom they would be most suited. A number of agencies are not involved in the assessment of mutual suitability when a particular child is proposed. An unsuited match could result in this situation.

4. *Final approval for bringing a child from abroad*

Not all countries have a central authority involved in the process of final approval. This authority is distributed among the various local bodies, such as county councils as well as private organizations. In the absence of such a body, the vital functions such as information channeling, assurance of compliance with the documental requirements of the countries involved, and general monitoring remain unattended. The overall functions of coordination, periodic review, and appropriate revision of policy and procedures also remain neglected.

5. *Immigration*

The function of the immigration authority with respect to the adoptive child's entry is not well coordinated with the

[4] T. G. Gunesekeran, Secretary to the Government, Ministry of Social Welfare, Sri Lanka.

adoption authority in some countries. The adoption authority, while issuing approval for the adoption placement to a certain family for a particular child, has not insured that the immigration authority would grant an entry permit to the child. This may result in the child being refused entry (particularly for health reasons), in spite of a relationship already having been established with the adoptive parents through legal measures in the child's country.

6. *Postplacement supervision*

While most adoption authorities uphold the importance of postplacement supervision, duration for such supervision varies from country to country. In most countries the same duration is applied for a transracial adoption as for in-country adoption without giving due consideration to the difficulties inherent in the adjustment process of a child from another culture and language, particularly when it concerns an older child. Moreover, in some countries, for example, the United States, adoption agencies do not necessarily have a commitment to provide postplacement services, even though they have been involved in the process of evaluation. The responsibility of following the placement through the completion of adoption remains unattended under this circumstance.

7. *Legitimation of adoption*

In this process a majority of the difficulties arise due to a difference in the concept of law (such as a customary law) and consequent lack of recognition in some countries of a legal measure erected in the child's country. This happens particularly in the case of immigrant adoptive parents, who travel to their native country and adopt a child. An adoption decree may be executed according to the local customary law, the child may start living with and developing a relationship with the adoptive parents, and then either the child is refused entry to accompany the new parents or, if allowed entry, he/she is not eligible for normal entitlements from the state, in the receiving country, that does not recognize customary adoption. This may leave the child without a name, a nationality, or a legal status in his new country.

POSSIBLE MEASURES

In consideration of the measures at each of the successive steps in the process of intercountry adoption, importance is attached to the feasibility aspect. The measures suited to different countries would ultimately depend upon various factors, such as the geographical and population size, sociopolitical structure, administrative infrastructures, incidence of desertion and destitution of children, level of welfare service provisions in general, and services for children in need of substitute care in particular. As there are wide variations and an admittedly wide gap in the knowledge and understanding of the prevailing practices in the different countries, the measures suggested here suffer from this limitation. Based on the assumption, again, that the sending countries represent a developing economy and the receiving countries a developed one, measures for the respective set of countries are discussed separately. This discussion is preceded by the general consideration of the role of national governments and of legislative provisions.

GOVERNMENT INVOLVEMENT IN INTERCOUNTRY ADOPTION PROGRAMS

It has been recognized as a sound guiding principle that in the broad national interest, governments should undertake the responsibility of promoting general family and child welfare and of insuring that established standards are observed in delivery of services. In considering the role of the national governments within the specific context of intercountry adoption, it is essential to recognize that the nature and the extent of governments' role in sending countries will differ from that in the receiving countries.

In many of the sending countries, inadequacies of national services for the child in "normal" circumstances engage concentrated efforts and attention of the governments. Hence, even while a government and the public at large are aware of the needs of the child in "special" circumstances, response to their needs generates insufficient interest. Against this backdrop are the practical considerations of the present service structures and their suitability.

"Formalized" services in personal, intimate areas of welfare such as child placement and family or marital counseling that require an individualized approach are still comparatively alien to the framework of a governmental system of public welfare services. By and large, direct government involvement in the majority of sending countries would seem contraindicated. Nevertheless, government's role is indispensable for continuous monitoring and insuring compliance with established standards and procedures by individuals and agencies that administer services to the children.

RECEIVING COUNTRIES

In the receiving countries there are already social agencies that specialize in dealing with individual, case method services in child and family welfare. Some have sanctions to act on behalf of the community, while others act directly within the public welfare system.

What is of key importance in these countries is the government's participation at a central, coordinating, and monitoring level. A system should be worked out at a central level for coordinating adoption activities; insuring maintenance of uniform, minimum standards in the whole process of adoption, and insuring assumption of state responsibility for a foreign child until such time as that child is legally integrated through adoption and secures citizenship.

LEGAL INSTRUMENT

One of the essential and helpful devices to safeguard the interests of the child and the family who unite in adoption across national boundaries would undoubtedly be an international law, in spite of the inherent limitations. The possibility and feasibility of bringing about such a legal instrument have been under examination over the past two decades. However, there are many difficulties along the path to realizing this goal, ranging from wide divergence in national legislation to a complete absence of legislation. It is increasingly realized that changes that can be expected in this regard have to be modest and realistic.

Adoption laws at the national level in the countries concerned are a logical step forward. However, here also a distinction needs to be drawn between the ideal and the attainable.

ADOPTION LAWS

Few countries among the sending ones have a complete absence of any legal provision for adoption. Others have some legal provision, but many of these are anachronistic. Where customary laws exist and govern child adoption, these laws may be divergent for different communities as in India; and these are based on traditional concepts of child adoption. They are in most cases devoid of considerations of the child's welfare.

Development of appropriate adoption laws in individual countries depends on the legislative machinery, which is normally the concern of government and parliament (that is, on public opinion expressed through the politically influential groups). Failure of some developing countries to revise, or to introduce a new, enlightened legislative instrument, can be attributed to some of the following reasons that are more frequently present in these countries. First, the concept of adoption in the modern context is still alien to these cultures. Second, there are excessive strains both on the available resources that can be employed in child and family welfare programs and on the legislative measures that are required to support them.

Hence, while keeping national and international legislation governing child adoption as a goal to be worked toward, other more feasible goals should be formulated in the interim period. Toward this purpose bilateral agreements should be worked out between the two countries involved in intercountry adoption. Some countries, such as Sweden and notably Australia, have undertaken the arduous task of setting up working agreements with different sending countries. A possible, bilateral measure should be considered. No adoption should be allowed unless a formal, working agreement is executed between the recognized authority—judicial or executive—in the child's country and a recognized adoption authority in the country of the adoptive family. This insistence could probably have the effect of generating enough pressures for formulating some definite regulations and procedures in both the countries.

MEASURES FOR SENDING COUNTRIES

ORGANIZATION OF CENTRAL ADOPTION RESOURCE AGENCY

Our review of the situation in the sending countries suggests that a network of agencies suitably distributed in different regions of the country and with a central office at the national level could provide information exchange and coordination of action on behalf of children who need permanent substitute homes. A central resource agency could facilitate in-country rehabilitation of children wherever possible. The resource agency should be organized at the national level, with suboffices suitably distributed at the regional levels, for providing information exchange and coordination of action.

ESTABLISHING ACCOUNTABILITY

Since the majority of children who are in need of care outside their family receive it in residential institutions, certain regulatory measures introduced at this level could serve to establish definite responsibility with the residential child care institutions. Statutory control could be placed over the rehabilitation plans followed by these institutions. Individual proposals independent of any institution's involvement may be disallowed. To serve these purposes the following recommendations should be considered:

1. All institutions providing residential care to minors should be required to obtain a license from the appropriate licensing authority instituted within the department responsible for child welfare matters.

2. The licensing requirement should be so defined as to insure certain minimum standards in the area of child care as well as rehabilitation programs.

3. All adoption proposals should be channeled through licensed and recognized institutions or other professional, specialized agencies dealing with family and child welfare work.

DETERMINING THE REAL STATUS OF THE CHILD

Given the current constraints in the developing countries the following measures could reduce possibilities of indiscriminate acceptance and subsequent placement by the concerned institutions.

1. All child care institutions (private or public) must be obliged to record a formal declaration, while receiving a child surrendered to the institution's care by an adult or by police who have taken charge of the minor. This declaration should contain identification information leading to the child's temporary or permanent abandonment. The institutions must maintain ongoing, detailed records of the child's changing circumstances.

2. All institutions receiving children in care must allow a lapse of a prescribed period of time before proposing a totally relinquished child for adoption. This time would provide for reconsideration of the guardian's decision. If a juvenile court is involved, the court must institute a process to insure that all efforts have been made to trace the child's antecedents.

3. No institution should be permitted to keep in its custody a child who is lost and found, without reference to the appropriate authority in an attempt to trace the antecedents of the child.

PLACEMENT

The primary responsibility of screening an adoption application and the assignment of a child should remain with the institution that is providing day-to-day care to the child. The staff resources and the other facilities at the disposal of many of the child care institutions being meager in the present circumstances, it would be unrealistic at this juncture to suggest that institutions employ professionally qualified staff to deal with adoption applications. It should be mandated that the institutions, after assigning a particular child to a particular family abroad, report the proposal to the licensing authority and obtain a no-objection certificate.

The proposed process could remain only a formality in the present circumstances, unless professional screening service at the level of a licensing authority is available, which may not be so in all cases. It could nevertheless serve as a check point in the process and may reduce the chances of irresponsible placements. A counterpoint is expressed to this suggestion. It is argued that it is tantamount to authorizing poor practices. It is agreed that the suggested measure would not serve the ideal purpose. Nevertheless, in the light of present realities, it could mark a step forward.

SELECTION PROCESS

The practice of accepting a general approval to bring in a foreign child for adoption should be modified so that approval would be acceptable only if it applies to a specific known child.

No application from a prospective adoptive family should be entertained unless the preadoptive requirements of a home evaluation and approval to bring in a foreign child for adoption, as well as assurance for postplacement supervision, have been met in the family's home country.

LEGITIMATION OF FOSTER PARENT-CHILD RELATIONSHIP

The process of legitimation of some kind of relationship between a child and his adopters (or prospective adopters) involves a higher, final authority in the child's country.

The legitimating authority should ask for regular assistance from a third party capable of an objective, expert evaluation of the proposal from both the legal as well as the welfare point of view. This third party must be an established agency with a good professional standing in the social welfare field.

Before the child is allowed to leave the country it must be assured that the guardianship of the child is assumed by a responsible authority in the government or an authorized agency of the receiving country.

Final adoption must follow in the receiving country after a stipulated period of preadoptive supervision.

EMIGRATION

In order to exercise some control over the emigration of minors who are unaccompanied by their natural parents, documents pertaining to the legal status of the child should be examined before issuance of a passport or travel document.

IN-COUNTRY REHABILITATION ALTERNATIVES

Indispensable to the development of national alternatives for children who cannot be cared for within their own family is the creation of wider public awareness and positive response to their needs. Efforts to promote in-country adoption meet with many odds; and the workers in this cause find themselves discouraged by the apparent lack of results or by painfully slow progress. International organizations could make a valuable contribution by lending their support to these activities.

National efforts for the promotion of in-country adoptions should receive assistance from the international agencies. This could be in the form of opportunities for mutual sharing of experiences and expertise at the national and the international levels where such efforts are already under way at local levels. Where in-country adoption promotion programs are totally absent, the initial thrust may be provided by an international agency, with its wider experience and expertise in the field.

The incidence of child desertion and destitution in the sending countries is very closely related to large-scale poverty, causing family disruptions resulting in desertion and neglect of children.

National governments must accord a priority to child and family welfare programs in their national development plans. Action programs must be progressively introduced and expanded to provide supportive aid to needy families and noninstitutional care for homeless children.

MEASURES FOR RECEIVING COUNTRIES

ORGANIZATION OF A CENTRAL ADOPTION RESOURCE AGENCY

A central adoption resource agency, a common measure, is suggested both for the sending as well as for the receiving countries.

Governments should organize a central, adoption monitoring and coordinating body at the national level to insure uniform, minimum standards of service within the country related to intercountry adoption; to liaise with foreign adoption authorities; and to discharge the state responsibilities relating to the child received in intercountry adoption.

ELIGIBILITY AND SUITABILITY CRITERIA

Eligibility criteria and standards applied in practice should as far as possible be made uniform within a country.

The standards applied to qualifying for intercountry adoption should be the same as those applied to in-country adoption.

A prospective family which is declared unsuitable for in-country adoption should not be permitted to adopt a child from abroad.

Adoptive evaluation must be done only by an authorized agency.

Evaluation by an independent practitioner should be disallowed unless endorsed by an authorized agency. Evaluation completed at the local agency level should be subject to approval by a higher authority in the government's child welfare department. Depending upon the size of the country, this approving body may also be at the regional government level and at the center. This approval should include a complete proposal of the particular child for the particular family. This higher authority should function in close coordination with the immigration authority to rule out any difficulties for the child's entry into the adoptive country at a later stage.

FINDING A CHILD

In order to minimize the scope for malpractice, and to reduce *ad hoc* or hasty placements, all adoption arrangements should be channeled through authorized agencies only, in both countries. Even when the prospective parents travel personally to select a child, their selection should be referred back to the adoption agency in their home country for approval. Money transactions should also be channeled through the agencies.

FINAL APPROVAL

Irrespective of the authorized agency that makes the homestudy assessment, as stated earlier, a higher authority within the department of child welfare at the central level should be involved in approving the family's request to bring in a particular child from abroad.

IMMIGRATION

An entry permit for the child should be given only after clearance from the final approving authority in the child's country is available.

LEGITIMATION, FOLLOW-UP, AND SUPERVISION

Among the numerous variations, the most satisfactory arrangement would be for families to complete preadoptive requirements in their own country and to receive the child on a preadoptive basis, through a guardianship release or on a provisional adoption order made in the child's country. The final legitimation of adoption should follow after a supervized period of satisfactory postplacement adjustment. Guardianship of the child should ideally remain with an authorized agency or an authority in a government department in the receiving country until completion of adoption. This provision would insure postplacement supervision and would insure protection to the child in case of placement breakdown or other crisis in the family that necessitates the child's removal.

Until final adoption is concluded, follow-up reports should be sent to the adoption authority in the child's country.

The supervision period should be a minimum of six months before final adoption is completed. In case of older and/or handicapped children, this period should be extended to a minimum of one year.

During the postplacement adjustment period, professional counseling should be made available to the family.

A new birth certificate or its equivalent should be filed in the child's adoptive family's name following the legal adoption, and steps must be taken to insure that the child acquires the nationality of the adoptive parents.

ROLE AND FUNCTIONS OF AN ADOPTION RESOURCE AGENCY

RECEIVING COUNTRIES

Some of the developed countries have already recognized the need for a central adoption unit, and this service is in the process of evolution. Canada and Norway have made a beginning in this direction. There is a definite need and scope for this service at a governmental level in the rest of the receiving countries. The main functions of such a unit should be:

1. Monitoring and channeling intercountry adoption documents between agencies within the country and foreign authorities and insuring that the required documentations are made in accordance with the procedural rules governing adoption in different countries
2. Coordination and liaison between individual agencies and authorities within and outside the country that are concerned with individual adoption placements.
3. Maintenance of a central registry, providing information exchange and policy guidance, such as organizing periodic reviews of policy and practices.

Adoption exchange. In addition to their role in intercountry adoptions, adoption resource agencies have an important role to play in in-country adoption. In the United States and the United Kingdom, where adoption resource exchanges started, their function was to facilitate the placement for adoption of children needing families within the country. This still remains an extremely important function for a central coordinating agency.

SENDING COUNTRIES

In sending countries, some of the functions of such a unit should be similar to those already listed in addition to others. The essential difference, however, would be in the area of authority and sanction. Here initiative and responsibility for developing such an unit cannot be assigned to the government for lack of equipment and resources at the disposal of the community and the government. The other consideration is that when responsibility is insisted on without the corresponding potential for its appropriate discharge, undesirable consequences inevitably follow. Hence, the role of a central adoption resource agency in developing countries may be conceived of as that of enabling rather than regulating, and its direction and guidance as coming from a voluntary sector. The aim should be to maximize the effectiveness of the existing services and provide for their improved functioning.

Residential child care institutions of varying sizes and resources that operate on a voluntary, informal basis provide a substantial part of the substitute child care services. These different individual resources form the backbone of the services. If undue restrictions or regulations are placed on their operation, the inevitable result would be discouragement and undermining of their contribution. Under the circumstances, the best strategy should be the development of complementary services that would act through facilitation rather than intrusion on the existing structures. The adoption resource agency could fill this role by providing the following services:

1. The single most important area of the agency's function in the initial stages should be the development of information resources. Building up thorough and complete information on all aspects of adoption and development of specialization and expertise should be the first task of such an agency.

2. Data exchange on children in need and parents who are

seeking to adopt within the country or from outside could be another invaluable service.

3. Direct assistance to the decision-making or sanctioning authority; that is, to the court or the executive adoption authority, before it grants final approval of an intercountry adoption proposal, would be useful.

4. The forum function of bringing about closer contact between independent institutions, agencies, and others from allied disciplines through organization of seminars and conferences could promote all-round better understanding and facilitate wider acceptance of the desired principles and practices.

5. Training facilities that offer opportunities for in-service continuing education in the specialized areas can also go a long way in the general overall improvement of adoption services.

Provision of an up-to-date information system does presuppose cooperation from all organizations that are concerned with family and child welfare services. This is difficult to elicit unless there is an authoritative base either derived from government sanction or developed by virtue of the utility and purposefulness of its functions. The latter kind of leadership role could be more desirable. This agency could endeavor to bring together qualified professionals and agencies with a view to building a lobby devoted to the cause of progressive, legislative, and other measures and to improve standards of services.

It might be unrealistic to expect the initiative to come from the governments in *some* of the developing countries for several reasons previously mentioned.

This presentation has sought to survey the scene of intercountry adoptions with a view to bringing out various issues that are of concern in the process of adoption across national lines. This document could not be sufficiently comprehensive or exhaustive to encompass all the issues or all the different variations in practices and procedures. It is hoped that future plans will be chalked out at this conference.

The national councils could undertake follow-up work in

this area in their respective countries. Acceptance and progressive implementation of the pertinent recommendations would require continuous and dynamic campaign activities at national levels.

Regarding the recommendations we have made, it may be noted that some measures would meet an intermediate goal rather than the ultimate one. Suggestions of a more modest goal in these cases are guided by the constraints in the present realities.

Development of Collaboration among Various Service Sectors at the Delivery Level

PART I

H. PHILIP HEPWORTH
ASSOCIATE PROFESSOR, UNIVERSITY OF REGINA,
REGINA, SASKATCHEWAN, CANADA

THE THEME of this conference may have been chosen for its timeliness for particular countries or groups of countries, but we should remember that the majority of mankind live out their lives in economic uncertainty. We face, therefore, a twofold challenge: poverty in all its manifestations, and uncertain or faltering prosperity, Just as we have coined the terms absolute and relative poverty, we should also think in terms of absolute and relative prosperity.[1] Whichever way we view prosperity, it is obvious that wealthier countries have long since passed the point of reasonable prosperity; gains beyond this point may be considered unreasonable or as merely relative gains. Just as we should seek a measure of equity between citizens within a country, we should seek a substantial measure of equity between countries. The route taken by most prosperous countries to achieve some greater degree of equity between their citizens has been towards a guaranteed minimum standard of living. I suggest that this is a worthwhile goal which we should strive to achieve for all citizens of the world. The reduction of poverty requires the regulation of prosperity; it requires action on both a national and an international level. The goal of social and economic development can thus be simply stated; its achievement may be a slow and tortuous process, yet it is still within the grasp of mankind.

[1] Peter Townsend, ed., *The Concept of Poverty* (London: Heinemann, 1970).

One's perception of economic uncertainty is of necessity culturally biased. Yet human needs are universal, and when due allowance has been made for social, cultural, political, and national differences, it is still possible to speak of similar needs and of the variety of ways used around the world to meet these needs. I shall approach the topic of collaboration of social service sectors—basically, the traditional social sectors, such as income security, health services, education, housing, employment services, and personal social services—recognizing that to some extent these terms are culturally specific. What we are concerned with, though, are examples of ways devised to meet basic human needs. The social inventions or institutions created for their purpose are not so important as their overall objectives. We are concerned with ways of achieving agreed social objectives and of overcoming constraints which often may be of our own making.

The achievement of minimum living standards for all people will require redistribution between rich people and poor people, between rich countries and poor countries. It will require changes of attitude on the part of deliverers of services. It will require an expanded awareness of what is possible. This measure of cooperation between people and peoples is possible, but it is not easily attained.

Collaboration between social service sectors may provide some examples of how this wider cooperation can and should be achieved. We may also discover why today we lay so much stress on such terms as coordination, integration, collaboration, cooperation. The root fact is that all our countries have been influenced by industrialization, by mass production, by specialization, and by the related professionalization. Titmuss made much the same observation twenty-four years ago at the VIIIth International Conference of Social Work: "Work has increasingly been split into smaller tasks by the demands of standardized mass production; human labour itself has come to be increasingly ruled by the clock, by the precision of the assembly line, the conveyer belt, and automation."[2]

[2] Richard M. Titmuss, "Industrialization and the Family," in *Essays on "The Welfare State"* (2d ed.; London: Unwin University Books, 1963), p. 109.

One of the consequences of this fragmentation of work has been the need to reintegrate the fragments, whether in a factory or an office, a hospital or a social services department. Such units or institutions serve also to perpetuate the division of labor and even to multiply it. In acknowledging the impact of industrialization on our lives, and recognizing that it has brought both benefits and costs, we should not idealize or romanticize the past. Subsistence living and hard manual labor were not and are not particularly life-enhancing; they lead to more of the same, what Titmuss called "the age-old passivity of agrarian poverty."[3] In fact, one of the challenges and goals for an international organization such as the ICSW is precisely to help poor people aspire to and gain a better life, one modeled on their own traditions and value systems, and not reflecting the imposed cultures of others.

It is obviously difficult for me to live up to these cautionary observations. I bring of necessity a particular set of cultural values and experiences from the United Kingdom, where I grew up, and from Canada, my country of adoption. I have had the benefit of participating in cross-national studies and in international forums, but it is still difficult to assume the posture of "disinterested attachment"[4] which Titmuss felt was needed for an international assignment of this kind. I belabor this point because I beieve it has relevance for the subject of collaboration. It is exceedingly difficult to refrain from imposing one's views, one's personal agenda, on other people.

Ideally, people come together voluntarily to collaborate on matters of mutual interest. Yet this mutual interest or benefit is often lacking when social service professionals and organizations work side by side. Specialization is a limiting process; restricted tasks and goals are set, and can be most easily accomplished, when complicating extraneous factors are ignored. It is often, for example, easier to treat the physical

---

[3] *Ibid.*, p. 104.

[4] ". . . our motives in desiring to fund and pass on the lessons of experience must have that quality of disinterested attachment on which empires, either of a material or an ideological kind, are assuredly not built." *Ibid.*, p. 106.

symptoms and injuries caused by child abuse than to make a thorough investigation of the child's family background.

I am aware that child abuse and the more restricted phenomenon of baby battering are culturally specific concerns which have surfaced in a number of highly prosperous countries. They are a reflection of social malaise and of an uneven distribution of life chances for children, even where the more obvious causes for restricted opportunities, such as poverty, poor housing, dirty water, and lack of basic health services are not present. Yet there is still good reason to believe that child neglect and abuse are related to poor living conditions in the prosperous countries. One can cite the Indians in Canada and the Maoris in New Zealand to support this contention.[5] Yet child abuse does occur in prosperous families, and this should alert us to a realization that prosperity alone is not sufficient for human happiness.

We may begin to see how our social service organizations relate to the intimate circumstances of human life, albeit imperfectly. We have devised rational structures, but the basis of our rationality is the nature of the activities performed within the organization, such as, for example, schools and hospitals, and not the target of our ministrations, the child, the adult, or the family.[6] The process of industrialization, the division of labor, and the growth of professional specialization have led logically to certain types of organizations. And try as we may with inter- or multidisciplinary teams, it is extremely difficult to get them working to the maximum benefit of the recipient of services, whether student, client, or patient.

What ways are there to improve this situation? The Canadian "Hall Commission" on health services reporting in the mid-1960s suggested that "in a world of specialists, it has become imperative to review and redefine the role of the general

---

[5] H. Philip Hepworth, *Foster Care and Adoption in Canada* (Ottawa: Canadian Council on Social Development, 1980); D. P. O'Neill et al., *Ex-nuptial Children and Their Parents; A Descriptive Survey* (Wellington, New Zealand: A. R. Shearer, Government Printer, 1976).

[6] Michael Rutter et al., *Fifteen Thousand Hours; Secondary Schools and Their Effects on Children* (Cambridge, Mass.: Harvard University Press, 1970).

practitioner."[7] This observation can be extended beyond the health services. In fact, we should perhaps ask whether what is needed are workers outside specific professional groupings, whose task it is to coordinate the provision of services for particular clients. Something of this idea is contained in Kahn's term "case integration."

The goal is continuity of service, consistency of stance, and concert of components. The rationale is simple: if one would undo what has resulted from a complex process of learning or socialization or development, only an internally consistent and mutually supportive series of actions of equal potency can be expected to make an impact.[8]

Where children have died as a result of abuse, official inquiries have revealed that a multitude of professionals, agencies, and private individuals have been involved and have had some degree of awareness that abuse was probably occurring. What has been seen repeatedly are tragedies of errors, errors of commission, omission, and sometimes of principle. What typically occurs during such inquiries is shifting of blame between the principal actors involved, the doctors, the teachers, the social workers, the agency administrators, the voluntary board members, and the elected politicians. This process is not a pleasant sight, but it repeatedly occurs. The legal question, "Quis custodiet custodes?" ("Who watches over the guardians?") is obviously applicable. The British Children Act 1975 makes provision for the appointment of a person whose responsibility is essentially that of an active watcher and guardian: "A guardian *ad litem* . . . shall be under a duty to safeguard the interests of the child or young person in the manner prescribed by rules of court."[9]

The principles involved in this provision would appear to have application in many settings. In this particular situation, the parent or legal guardian, who may be the official agency or government involved, is in effect seen to be no longer fully

---

[7] Canada, *Royal Commission on Health Services,* Vol. II (Ottawa: Roger Duhamel, Queen's Printer and Controller of Stationery, 1965), p. 259.
[8] Alfred J. Kahn, *Theory and Practice of Social Planning* (New York: Russell Sage Foundation, 1969), pp. 282–83.
[9] Elizabeth II c. 72, Children Act 1975, Section 64.

capable of operating in the best interests of the child. What is involved is the imposition of accountability on people or agencies not previously fully accountable for their actions.

The rapid introduction in many parts of the world of commissioners of human rights and of ombudsmen as watchdogs over government agencies reflects again some of the imperfections in our professionalized and bureaucratized institutions. But by their very nature these are "after-the-fact" operations, and what is needed are arrangements that insure that appropriate services are provided when and where and to whom they are needed.

What we are seeing, therefore, are piecemeal improvements of the institutional system. These improvements do not apply equally to all levels of government, to all agencies, or to all professions. It is not obvious that the self-policing arrangements of different professional groups adequately meet the need for public accountability. Yet governments have often been reluctant to regulate effectively some of the older and stronger professions.

It is obvious that general practitioners in various professions act as gatekeepers and regulate access to specialists. It is not always obvious that they have the knowledge and the competence to recognize their own limitations. General practitioners can thus be both facilitators and impediments. The client or seeker of services is thus often left frustrated, with his needs, as he perceives them, still unmet.

It is a fact that the layman, the seeker, the would-be user of services often has to diagnose and define his own needs and be his own case coordinator or integrator. This arrangement may or may not work well. It presupposes the ability to find one's way through the system. It gives the advantage to the educated, intelligent, well-off person. It is a system that is found surprisingly often even in the welfare states of today.

The issue of access to services as a problem is applicable both to specific service sectors and between service sectors. It is also a problem that is recognized in many countries. An expert group, meeting under the auspices of the United Nations European Social Development Program in Washington in October 1979, studied at some length methods of improving access to social services. The group concluded that continuing attention at the international level was warranted: "In the realm of social care the international affinities may often be greater than the national differences and this should be a matter of direct and continuing relevance to the United Nations Economic and Social Council."[10]

On the basis of the information and experiences shared, the group found that,

> barriers to access do not always arise inadvertently or by chance; although a service has a clear, beneficial intention, its purpose may be controversial and be shared neither by the staff who administer it nor by members of the public. In such circumstances the barriers cannot be readily removed by instituting administrative changes. A more positive approach, possibly involving an advocacy system, may be necessary to strengthen the power of clients and claimants in their interaction with the administration of the services.[11]

One can cite many examples of restricted access. In one Canadian province a senior official told me recently that as part of a general economy drive some 14 percent of social work positions were not being filled. One may ask, then, how such statutory duties as child protection can be adequately discharged. Canada has universal medical insurance, but the payment systems are such that there is a strong financial incentive for doctors either to overbook, to see a very large number of patients in a given time, or to underbook, seeing fewer patients and making a surcharge. In either case access to services is being restricted.

If there are these constraints within a particular social service sector, it is obvious that they also exist between sectors. A whole set of circumstances can facilitate or impede collaboration. One of the realizations that may be reached, perhaps reluctantly, by social service professionals is that our behavior

---

[10] UN office, Geneva, Division of Social Affairs, European Social Development Program, Summary of Report of Expert Group on Methods of Improving Access to Social Services, Washington, D.C., 1979, "Conclusions," p. 6. SOA/SEM/75/6 Rev. GE 79-5095.

[11] *Ibid.*, p. 9.

within organizational structures is likely to resemble that of any group of people in any type of organization. We are likely to arrange circumstances to our own advantage. Our professional codes of ethics may not be sufficiently strong to enable us to withstand and ignore considerations of personal advantage and convenience. I am not saying that codes of ethics are not important, but it is necessary to pay attention to potential conflicts of interest and to create appropriate accountability mechanisms. We should acknowledge our human frailty.

On a more optimistic level it is apparent that social service sectors vary from country to country, and from time to time. Organizational arrangements differ, and it is these differences that suggest ways in which things can be rearranged in our own countries. The care of preschool children is strikingly different even between countries in the same part of the world. In some countries a minimal, social service type of care is provided for priority groups of children; in other countries, virtually all children over the age of two receive early childhood education programs. There is thus the opportunity for comparison, for change, and for progress.

We do not have to accept rigid demarcation between social service sectors. For example, in countries where there is a declining child population, it is obvious that much fuller use could be made of schools as community service centers and adult education facilities. There is all the more argument for using community facilities for a multiplicity of activities when economic resources are restricted. I am fairly certain that this type of inventiveness is practiced widely in many countries where professional and departmental boundaries have not solidified. In pioneering days in the United States it was a common practice to erect a building that served as both church and school. We need this type of flexibility again.

Titmuss spoke once of a blurring of demarcation lines between types of care, between diagnostic labels attached to children, and between types of need. He saw this as "all part of a general movement toward more effective service for the public and toward a more holistic interpretation and operational definition of the principles of primary, secondary and tertiary prevention."[12]

He went on:

> On a broader plane, society is moving toward a symbiosis which sees the physician, the teacher and the social worker as social service professionals with common objectives. . . . The health, education and social work (personal welfare) services are . . . all concerned with the individual and the family, and all concerned with his mental, physical and social development. They all have in common a concern for prevention, early case-finding and early mobilization of a network of specialized services with responsibilities for therapy and treatment.[13]

No man was better qualified than Titmuss to understand the constraints within modern societies which prevent the full realizaton of the goals and ideals he exemplified. But whether he was talking about Britain or Canada, the United States, Mauritius, or Tanzania, he always kept in view what was practically possible in meeting human needs. We need again his idealism and his humorous dismissal of human cynicism.

In seeking collaboration between social service sectors, we are looking for ways of overcoming constraints. We are looking for ways in which we can transcend our narrow specialties. We are looking for people, and not for categories, diseases, and disabilities. Financial restraints and cutbacks have raised again the specter of residualism in social services. We hear again the specious arguments for selectivity, for targeting programs and value for money. But selectivity without universality is a false economy; if we choose to go this route we turn the clock back, and do so at our peril.

I mentioned the problems that the individual citizen faces in gaining access to services. Increased selectivity will make access even more difficult. A basis of universality in social services permits access to more specialized services for those who need them. Universality is an acknowledgment of common human needs. It is a principle that is worth fighting for, it is

---

[12] Richard M. Titmuss, "The Welfare Complex in a Changing Society," in *Commitment to Welfare* (New York: Pantheon Books, 1968), p. 73.
[13] *Ibid.*, pp. 73–74.

a principle that pays due respect to human dignity, and which applies across the arbitrary boundaries of our social service sectors.

THE INTERNATIONAL PERSPECTIVE

There is some symmetry between the need for collaboration between social service sectors and between all social and economic sectors within the modern welfare state—what Myrdal calls the "organizational state"[14]—and the need for collaboration between modern nation states. Using agriculture as an example of the type of international coordination and harmonization required if we really wish to reintegrate the world economy, Myrdal argues:

The need to avoid international disintegration as a result of the agricultural policies of individual countries should be faced as a common concern. If there were a basis of international solidarity approaching in strength the existing national one, it should be possible to reach international agreement on national agricultural policies in the several countries. These policies might be different, but would nevertheless be so harmonized that they did not, as now, lead simply to a competition between the countries to shift their burdens onto each other.[15]

Relationships between countries are, if anything, more regulated by conventions, international rules, than are the relationships between social service sectors and professions within nations. Yet there are some examples of cooperation on the international level which give some reason for hope both at the national and the international level. I think principally of the World Health Organization, but there are many other examples relating to children, refugees, and famine relief.

Despite his optimism Myrdal sounds a warning note:

As was the case in the individual welfare states when they moved towards closer national integration, so in the world at large this process of international integration would need the impetus of economic progress. Only in a rapidly and steadily expanding world economy would there exist the conditions for mutual generosity.[16]

[14] Gunnar Myrdal, *Beyond the Welfare State* (New York: Bantam Books, 1967), p. 144.
[15] *Ibid.*, p. 145.
[16] *Ibid.*

Myrdal goes on to argue that the goals of the national welfare state can only be built in the wider world community if our old ideals of liberty, equality, and brotherhood are attained:

> When once the national welfare state has come into existence and built its moorings firmly in the hearts of the peoples who in the democracies of the western world have the political power, there is no alternative to international disintegration except to begin, by internatioal cooperation and mutual accommodation, to build the welfare world.[17]

These remarks seem as valid today as they were when they were written.

I depart from Myrdal's analysis on only one point. Is mutual generosity necessarily predicated on economic growth nationally and internationally? One of the few beneficial lessons of war is that civilian populations can and do pull together, ration scarce resources cooperatively, and fight for common goals—that is, if there is not a total breakdown of government and morale.[18]

In times of economic uncertainty we need more cooperation between social service sectors, between all sectors of a nation's economy, and between all nations of the world, between rich and poor. We tend to forget the progress we have made and the progress we can still make. I believe we can and should transcend our professional and national boundaries. We should be proud of our idealism and dream a few dreams.

---

[17] *Ibid.*, p. 147.
[18] Richard M. Titmuss, "War and Social Policy," in *Essays on "The Welfare State,"* pp. 75–87; Richard M. Titmuss, *Problems of Social Policy*, (London: His Majesty's Stationery Office, 1950).

PART II

MOACYR VELLOSO CARAOSO DE OLIVEIRA
CENTRO BRASILEIRO DE COOPERACAO E INTERCAMBIA DE
SERVICOS SOCIAIS, BRAZILI

IN ORDER to achieve collaboration we must honestly answer four main questions:
 Why is collaboration necessary?
 Who should collaborate?
 Why do people resist collaboration?
 How do we achieve collaboration?

WHY IS COLLABORATION NECESSARY?

Society is built through cooperation among its members, and lack of collaboration makes peace difficult. As social beings, men must interact with their fellow creatures. This process, to be a gratifying one, should have a cooperative approach in order to bring people together. To collaborate, people must be near each other and must act through complementary forms of behavior, thus generating new collaborative processes.

Technical reasons are also to be considered. For clients, collaboration results in a more global achievement of their individual needs. For social agencies, collaboration means new opportunities for in-service training, thus leading to a better quality of services. And we must not forget the financial importance of collaboration.

WHO SHOULD COLLABORATE?

It is not unusual to think of collaboration among social agencies as a process in which only staff members and clients should be involved. However, in order to be effective, the process should also include collaboration among staff members. Of course, clients should also collaborate among themselves.

Social agencies should function in an integrated system in which the actions of each staff member and/or client complement each other. The dichotomy between agents and clients must be changed into a system in which agents and clients work together with the same goals in mind.

WHY DO PEOPLE RESIST COLLABORATION?

Despite all its advantages, our everyday life proves that it is not easy to live in collaboration. It is better to recognize resistance than to attempt to ignore it.

REASONS FOR COLLABORATION

Social reasons. Society is built on such closed and organized groups that the survival of some seems directly dependent on the failure of others. Many times a close relationship between people and groups aims at the destruction of others. This may be observed at the international level as well as at national, regional, and institutional levels and even at family and individual levels.

The history of so-called civilizations shows that cooperative processes emerge mainly when groups must face common enemies. This observation does not apply solely in times of war. A Brazilian senator, Nelson Carneiro, says that he succeeded in having the divorce law passed because many groups were against him; now that he is trying to introduce laws that will benefit elderly people he fails because everybody agrees with him.

Is man such an unreasonable being that he knows how to make friends only when there is a common enemy to be destroyed? Shall we have to wait for people from another planet to invade the earth for humanity to be united?

We should also consider that society is divided into social classes in both developed and in developing countries. This makes communication between those in very different positions a difficult process. Theoretically, social structure means only social differences between groups of social classes. In practice, social classes isolate themselves, and those in very different positions feel as though they were at opposite poles.

Modern urban society is also responsible for social isolation. The urbanization processes produce conglomerations which, in turn, lead to isolation, lack of communication, and therefore to lack of collaboration.

The study of groups shows that competitive processes are more frequent among group members and engender more enthusiasm and participation.

What about sports clubs? According to our observations, they are not concerned, at least basically, with the welfare of their members. They are much more concerned with finding good athletes who can represent them in competitions and at the Olympic games. Those who are able to win medals and cups are chosen and well paid.

And the family? So far as we know, the family is the only existing group built on the basis of love. Therefore, the family should be a friendly society. But it is not unusual to find families whose members develop hostile feelings toward one another, and yet try to preserve outward appearances.

School and work are also good examples of competitive systems.

Social agencies' reasons. Apart from the more general reasons, others are found in the social agencies themselves. They exist in a social context and reflect the social environment in which they exist. Despite the fact that they try to correct social malfunctioning, they reflect social malfunctioning.

One also has to consider that for practical reasons agencies must define their clients. While dealing with people according to special criteria, agencies become more and more specialized, and cooperation between agencies that have very different goals becomes difficult if not impossible.

Administrative procedures too seem to interfere with collaborating processes. It is not unusual to find bureaucracy defeating collaboration in private as well as in official and semiofficial agencies.

Staff members' personal reasons. Personal reasons of those who are responsible for services rendered favor the creation of resistance processes against collaboration. There are many, and they may be found in isolated as well as in combined forms.

It may be interesting to mention the self-image of those who should render services. It is not unusual for staff members to consider themselves in a higher social position than their clients. This feeling interferes with their communication patterns, creating an artificial and vertical structure which does not help task performance on a cooperative basis.

Another common personal reason is the search for social activities as a means of personal satisfaction. Social agencies are seen as places where people without personal goals can go regularly as volunteers. Such people are more concerned with themselves than with the well-being of the needy. These are frequently unconscious processes. Clients become the means by which their benefactors are served, and cooperative processes are likely to emerge mainly among those who are there to offer help. In other words, the benefits of help tend to fall mainly among service renderers, but clients receive at least the material results of the work performed by others.

Compensation induces people to join social programs. Their aims are quite different from those officially recognized. In social agencies with specific goals, it is not unusual to find people who face in their private lives the same problems that trouble their clients. Under such conditions, these volunteers are much more concerned with their own fate than with their clients' problems. We cannot minimize their contribution, but we cannot forget that their prevailing reasons are based on strong emotional motives that frequently lead to negative approaches in rendering service.

Another personal reason is lack of interest in task performance. The social field is increasingly being professionalized. This, of course, favors the presence of well-trained personnel but, on the other hand, lack of opportunities in the labor market leads professionals to accept jobs in institutions whose goals do not correspond to their individual inclinations. In such cases, financial reasons are more important than personal ones, and the social aspects are hindered.

It is also important to remember that frequently those in charge of rendering services do not have a clear understanding of social problems; they fight against consequences because they do not know the roots of the problems that affect society as a whole.

Clients' personal reasons. The very fact that they are received as people in need of help—seems responsible for latent feelings of inferiority that may lead clients to revolt against their own situation. The self-image thus created is not a favorable one and, of course, does not encourage collaboration.

On the other hand, administrative procedures, geographical distance, financial problems, low level of schooling, and many other obstacles are also responsible for clients' lack of enthusiasm for collaborating in programs of the social agencies that receive them.

HOW DO ALL ACHIEVE COLLABORATION?

Recognizing the need for collaboration, accepting that staff members as well as clients should collaborate, and knowing that resistance processes exist both in society and in human beings, we must work with human beings in such a way that they may change, and then become able to change society, making collaboration possible and effective. In this changing process we cannot forget ourselves.

We should start by asking ourselves whether we know how to accept collaboration, how to ask for collaboration, how to offer collaboration. These three things seem to be very easy. However, they are difficult and complex. Many and many times they lead to resentment and conflict among those who are involved in the process.

We should also consider our working methods: do they favor collaboration among social agencies, staff, and clients? If those answers are not affirmative, we cannot work in collaboration.

Lastly, we must ask ourselves whether our administrative procedures *allow* social agencies, staff, and clients to collaborate.

If we have very precise and clear answers to these and many

other questions, we shall be on the way to reaching our target. Only then shall we have the means to achieve the collaboration of an increasing number of people. It will then be accepted as a living process, a risky process, in which conflicts will arise, a process filled with unpredictable incidents, a process that always begins again and hopefully is unending—a life system to be daily improved—undoubtedly a difficult task but also a gratifying one. This is, of course, a personal task.

As professionals, we shall be able to introduce changes in our working methods so that many people can collaborate and create administrative procedures that allow—and even demand—wholehearted collaboration. We can also bring agents and clients closer together so that a new system of working emerges and contributes to theoretical reformulations. We can so work that our clients help society to change. It is in interpersonal and social relationships that each of us becomes capable of analyzing and changing the society in which we coexist.

The René Sand Award

GETTING BACK TO PEOPLE: A BID FOR A NEW APPROACH

GRADUS HENDRIKS

DIRECTOR-GENERAL FOR SOCIAL DEVELOPMENT, MINISTRY OF CULTURAL AFFAIRS, RECREATION, AND SOCIAL WELFARE, NETHERLANDS

FIRST OF all I wish to thank all those who have made it possible for me to receive the René Sand Award today. I accept this honor in all humility. All of us who are at home in the field of social welfare know how many others there are who are worthy of this award. It has become a sound tradition that on evenings such as this the opportunity is offered to present one's views on social welfare. In choosing my subject I have taken account of the widely varied company attending this conference. We all come under the common heading of social welfare, but the work which we do is often of a highly divergent nature. Yet there is one fundamental point which binds us all together, whatever our nationality or cultural background, and that is our interest and involvement in the welfare of the individual in his own local community. That social commitment and that motivation are the bond between us.

In the light of this bond I propose that we look at the people who set significant social developments in motion at the local level, often as volunteers or ordinary citizens working behind the scenes. Thus my theme is "getting back to people." What opportunities are there to give these workers, whether amateur or professional, more material and moral support?

A second motive in selecting my subject was the fact that 1980 is a special year. This year there will be a special session of the United Nations General Assembly for the 1980s, and the UN is devoting special attention to the social sector.

I shall first outline the objectives and the means which have been evolved at the international level.

There is then the question of what has been achieved in terms of those objectives, and the present position in both developing and developed countries.

The next question is whether it is still possible to initiate an effective course of development for the 1980s.

Finally, I should like us to consider ways in which we can provide more opportunities for social development at the local level. For it is at this level where we meet the people with whom we are concerned. What is needed here is not declarations, resolutions, or well-produced reports, but practical ideas about the scope, both material and social, which can be provided at the local level.

OBJECTIVES AND MEANS DEVISED AT WORLD LEVEL

Over the past few decades increasing attention has been paid to the social and human aspects of development questions in the various international forums in addition to the more political and economic aspects. Since the establishment of the UN in 1945 numerous resolutions, declarations, and conventions relating in all sorts of ways to global standards and objectives in human welfare have been adopted in these forums: the alleviation of poverty; better health care and nutrition; literacy programs; and special welfare measures for specific population groups such as women, children, youth, the handicapped, the elderly, and migrants. All these are now generally accepted objectives which form a continuous thread throughout many UN resolutions and decisions. The 1969 United Nations Declaration on Social Progress and Development and the international development strategy for the Second Development Decade are notable in this respect.

Over the past twelve years UN conferences have been held on social welfare (1968), human environment (1972), population (1974), women (1975), settlements (1976), and employment (1976). At all these conferences world plans of action were adopted which expressed a desire to involve the population actively in the formulation, implementation, and evaluation of local-level action programs for improving the quality of human existence. In this same period the UN produced new development concepts and models such as the comprehensive approach, the unified approach to development analysis and planning, the basic needs strategy, ecodevelopment, and a new international economic order. In all of these the emphasis was constantly placed on social equality and justice.

The means to achieve objectives at the world level, however, remained limited. Often it was more of a paper factory than a real action program. Nor were technical and financial aid suitably adapted to rapidly changing situations, particularly in the case of young countries, to enable them to build up their administrations in the social field as elsewhere. This situation is best described in the words of Ernst Michaneck, Director-General of the Swedish International Development Authority, who said:

> It simply says that the strategies have not been followed by the action that they presuppose and that therefore they may have been *useless* or even *counterproductive*. . . . I cannot remember having met one developing country spokesman who has referred to them as of importance to his country's planning of performance.[1]

GENERAL

I fully realize that the worth of declarations and resolutions adopted in one or other UN context can be no more than relative. They are, as it were, an expression by the member states (the world community) of a common feeling and a common will to strive for a particular goal. The national governments of member states of the UN are often insufficiently aware of the hopes that are awakened by the launching of these often very appealing ideas. Hopes which are unfulfilled are an additional burden to the people who need our assistance. This is not the place for a detailed analysis of the reasons for the failure of international development policy in recent years. I merely offer a few possible explanations:

[1] *Development Forum* (1979), vol. 7, no. 8.

1. International declarations are too broadly formulated. This leads to problems of identification in specific situations, groups, and countries.

2. Approaches to the analysis and alleviation of need are still too often keyed to situations and frames of reference in developed countries.

3. I also seriously wonder whether views on development policy at the world level do not shift too radically. Can member states, administrations, social groups, and particularly individuals, really assimilate all these changes so quickly?

4. There is also the problem that nations are given too little of the kind of technical and financial support they need to enable them to make a start themselves, in their own way, with the implementation of important concepts and resolutions.

I must point out here that three quarters of the UN budget is paid out in salaries: in salaries, I might even venture to say, that often stand out in painful contrast to the living conditions of those who are the daily concern of UN staff.

I further refer you to the interesting publication of the UN Research Institute for Social Development, "Social Development and International Development Strategy."[2]

So what is our present position? Arriving at the balance with regard to the developing countries, we get the following picture.

DEVELOPING COUNTRIES

Parallel to the reconstruction of the developed countries after 1945 ran the process of decolonization, whereby the newly emerging nations embarked upon large-scale industrialization and urbanization programs. The establishment of modern industrial settlements was accompanied by heavy migration from rural areas to urban centers, with the unfortunate consequence that the self-supporting rural areas became impoverished and new urban elites emerged, together with extensive slum areas in the cities.

[2] UN Research Institute for Social Development, Geneva, 1979.

The welfare of the people became one of the major goals in the constitution of every developing country. Objectives and policy measures to promote welfare were set out in five-year plans concentrated on various sectors. To bridge the gap between backward rural areas and urban standards, community development programs were set up in the 1950s. These programs were, however, too heavily biased toward welfare and Western ideas, and they did not have the desired effect for poor farmers and craftsmen.

In the 1960s the rich countries began to show signs of what has been termed "development aid weariness." As a result of this and other factors the aided countries were more or less compelled to call a premature halt to, or to cut back on, their ambitious social programs and to concentrate their attention and their resources on the most pressing national problems, such as food shortages, natural disasters, and economic problems of all kinds.

The 1970s were characterized by economic stagnation, shifts of political power, and social unrest. Though it is true that the self-awareness of the man in the street is gradually increasing, the silent majority still remains beyond the reach of development efforts. This is due, among other things, to powerlessness, a lack of political interest, and the dualism arising from the emergence of a small minority of new elite groups with know-how, money, and power while the bulk of the population lives in poverty.

Applying science and technology to increase food production and provide energy has not improved the lot of the very poor. The so-called green revolution remains a distant dream for the small farmer in Asia, Africa, South and Central America. Fortunately, substantial progress has been made toward achieving self-reliance and improving living standards, but the rapid population growth in many countries has again greatly increased the burden. The fact that large groups of people have been left outside the scope of development efforts continues to be a major problem.

DEVELOPED COUNTRIES

There have been three distinct phases in the European welfare state since 1945, as has been set out in the German report for the ICSW conference.[3]

The first phase, the reconstruction period (1945–50), was characterized by efforts to meet basic needs, motivated by a deep-seated conviction that a sound economic policy is at the same time the best social development policy.

The second phase (1950 to the early 1970s) was devoted to the establishment and development of the welfare state. It was based on economic, social, and cultural growth and characterized by government guarantees and financing of a minimum wage, job opportunities, social security, health care, education, and other facets of social and cultural welfare. The guiding principle of social policy in this phase was "welfare for all."

In the third phase (1973 onward), we have come face to face with the painful question of the limits to growth. The uncertainties of the 1980s affect developed countries not only in terms of their economic and financial position, but socially and culturally as well. The social aspect is represented in the welfare state by extensive provisions for social security, health care, education, and social services for the entire population, with additional attention being devoted to population groups requiring special services or assistance.

The financial management of these welfare facilities, which have assumed vast proportions in the last fifteen years, poses major problems now that economic growth is practically at a standstill. As the regional report for Europe explains in great detail, the economic recession has prompted attempts to gear welfare provisions more closely to the real needs of the population by establishing more clear-cut criteria and priorities.

Unfortunately, it must also be said that despite the extended welfare bureaucracies there are still yawning gaps in the care provided and a weakened human approach. The underlying causes for both our social and our economic problems are, in

---

[3] Regional Report for Europe, Middle East, and Mediterranean Area, ICSW Conference, Hong Kong, 1980.

my opinion, rooted in an ideological crisis, a lack of a sense of purpose and real prospects for betterment in people's lives. In the recent Organization for Economic Cooperation and Development (OECD) "Interfutures" study this is referred to as the absence of a "grand design." Such a design existed in 1945, in the reconstruction period, but has now practically disappeared.[4]

The Danish Ambassador to the Netherlands, Tyge Dahlgaard, a man with wide experience in international affairs, considers reorientation to be an essential social task awaiting fulfillment. He is of the opinion that, given the problems confronting the world, emphasis must henceforth be placed on people's "personal sense of responsibility" because in our efforts to achieve a purposeful existence we may already have gone beyond the optimal point.[5] For this reason, too, I feel that in our search for a new sense of purpose we in the developed countries must turn our attention once again to people themselves in their own living and working environment.

INTERNATIONAL DELIBERATIONS ON FURTHER DEVELOPMENT

Social development is a primary responsibility of each individual nation which, given the political will, can achieve a great deal. However, an international conference cannot ignore what is happening at the world level.

The year 1980 is a special year: we are now moving into the third development decade and formulating ideas about a "new international economic order" and a "new international development strategy." At the end of August, 1980, that is to say, a special session of the UN General Assembly is to be held to discuss these issues. I think it would be proper for the ICSW to add its voice to the debate by expressing its views on the social development element.

---

[4] "There is the absence of a grand design that represents the consensus of society," in *Interfutures. Facing the Future, Mastering the Probable, and Managing the Unpredictable* (Paris: OECD, 1979).

[5] *Nieuwe Rotterdamse Courant,* April 12, 1980.

I also wish to make several observations about UN activities in the past few years in the social field:

Formerly, social development planning and the social welfare sector were housed under one roof in New York. Over the years a considerable degree of constructive interaction was built up between the two. After the reorganization of the UN Secretariat, however, the Center for Social Development and Humanitarian Affairs was deprived of two of its previous areas of activity, namely, planning and technical assistance, and was transferred with its reduced work load to Vienna. Member states have registered uneasiness at the reorganization and the dislocation this entailed. In 1979 the Economic and Social Countil (ECOSOC) adopted a resolution in which an ad hoc group of independent persons was requested to report on the social aspects of UN development activities.[6] I had the pleasure of being one of that group.

The ad hoc group recognized that the social aspects of development should be viewed within the broad context of a unified approach to development and a new international economic order. At the same time, strong emphasis was placed on the promotion of a "people-oriented development process" and on the idea of processes proceeding from the base upward, which was the inspiration for the theme, "getting back to people."

The report of the group also includes many practical recommendations for better coordination and cooperation among the main agencies of the UN responsible for social development policy. The report furthermore urges that the work of the UN center in Vienna be more clearly defined and that it be given wider scope for field operations. In addition, the functioning of the Commission for Social Development should be improved for the third decade.

The ad hoc group also made recommendations for nongovernmental organizations—including, of course, the ICSW—which can contribute not only to the wide dissemination of

[6] ECOSOC Resolution 1979/45 of May 11, 1979.

ideas, but also to the implementation of resolutions and reports.

For further information I refer you to the report.[7] We have adopted the motto of "action from the base"; now we ourselves are required to take action.

THE WAY AHEAD

Progress over the next few years will be determined by the amount of consideration given to the following points:
1. The common will of people to achieve a new international economic order
2. The responsibility which nations will be willing to accept for both economic and social development
3. The willingness of governments to take people as their point of departure, with local development and encouragement of the active involvement of the population of prime importance.

For more information about the first two aspects I refer you to the Brandt Report which has recently been published in connection with the next development decade.[8] I shall dwell briefly on the last point, with emphasis on people themselves.

In my analysis I stated that for various reasons we must get back to people if we are to solve our problems. For this purpose local development is important; for it is at the local level that we find people in their own social and cultural environment, with their own needs and aspirations. Their active participation cannot be viewed separately from the local situation.

Voluntary organizations as well as governments, specifically those active in the social field, can fulfill an important supportive function in local development and in involving the local

---

[7] "Social Development Questions," report of the ad hoc working group on the social aspects of the development activities of the UN. E/1980/31; 15.04.1980 ECOSOC.

[8] "North–South: a Program for Survival," Report of the Independent Commission on International Development Issues under the chairmanship of Willy Brandt (London: Pan Books, 1980).

population in activities. Let me first take the situation in developed countries, since perhaps it is precisely there that we might learn how *not* to proceed in developing countries.

In Western countries we usually find a democratic form of government with very extensive and still-growing governmental machinery, and many services and institutions run by professional staff. The influence of the ordinary citizen and his participation in decision-making and in effecting improvements in the management of services are dwindling steadily. Groups of people of all kinds object to this situation. They want to take part in the planning and management of the facilities provided for their benefit. People also try to influence decision-making and the day-to-day conduct of affairs by means of campaigns and pressure groups.

Despite our material prosperity there is a growing feeling of malaise. People no longer feel that they are a part of their own living and working environment, and want more opportunity to influence their situation and to do something about it themselves.

What attempts have been made in Western Europe to meet these demands?

1. Citizens have more influence in the running of important institutions, such as universities, industrial enterprises, and the large voluntary organizations.

2. The clients themselves, the voluntary and the professional workers, have more say in the management of social welfare organizations.

3. There are more opportunities for ordinary citizens to determine the form and content of their own welfare requirements and activities (self-organization).

4. The present policy is to encourage people to take an active part in community life.

5. Power and financial resources have been delegated from the national to the local level (United Kingdom, Denmark, Poland, the Netherlands).

Many people feel that these improvements do not go far enough toward satisfying their demands. They often wish to be personally involved at the local level, to do more than merely express their views. They must be given wider scope for action if this is to be achieved.

The material means are often available, but government control of the practically complete range of welfare provisions gives people insufficient opportunity to make their own personal contribution or to carry any personal responsibility.

What is the situation in the developing countries, and what can be learned from the picture I have just presented?

The national administrations in many newer countries had to be built up or adapted after decolonization. Local administrative machinery was weak or practically nonexistent. In some cases the people's own forms of local self-government had been disrupted or repressed in the past. For the development of the country as a whole in many different areas it was necessary to strengthen the national machinery, often at the expense of the local authorities. We have witnessed a similar trend in Western Europe, where we are now laboriously seeking the way back to the more personal level. For this reason I plead that attention be devoted to all facets of local development.[9]

In the early 1970s the idea of a unified approach to development analysis and planning was introduced to the international community.[10] This new approach placed greater emphasis than before on the importance of popular participation in development programs. Since then, UN publications have been filled with references to this idea. Here again we are faced with the question of whether this new trend is not based too heavily on Western concepts that accentuate the importance of having a say in decision-making processes. Very often the authorities devise the plans, and the public only have an opportunity for active participation in discussions at the second stage.

In developing countries advantage is taken of the willingness of individuals to be active in their own living and working

---

[9] The Rome meeting of the Society for International Development held on February 23, 1980, urged upon its members to link all programs to the local level (*Compass*, no. 5, 1980).

[10] See General Assembly Resolution 3409-(XXX) of November 28, 1975.

environments. This I refer to as "active individual social involvement."

Small population groups (villages, communes, and so on) gradually build up a better existence according to their wishes and needs. What may then be required of the authorities in certain cases is to give a more concrete form to these efforts. It may also be necessary to assess them against the background of more broadly based interests.

In this context I remind you of what E. F. Schumacher says in his work *Small Is Beautiful*.[11] His premise is that economic development is dependent on four essential conditions: motivation, some know-how, some capital, and, finally, an outlet. I would emphasize the words "some know-how" and "some capital." Appropriate technology has shown how much practical knowledge and experience people often possess. Schumacher also says that progress should not be an end in itself, but that there should be progress in the local and national community, geared to fundamental human standards and not to the growth concept of the West. Only then can people be liberated and progress to a satisfactory level of development.

If I combined these thoughts and made a comparison with the situation which has arisen in Western-oriented countries, I would formulate the following guiding principles for local development *by* the people:

1. Local development by the people themselves must be focused primarily on their immediate basic needs.

2. Given the scarcity of capital goods, use must also be made of local endeavors, technical knowledge and experience (appropriate technology).

3. For the same reasons, the ideas and requirements of the people themselves must be taken as the starting point (self-determination).

4. The nature of projects and the pace at which they are carried out must be determined by the people themselves.

5. The role of specific groups within the community, such as youth and women, can greatly be enhanced. I hope, inci-

---

[11] E. F. Schumacher, *Small Is Beautiful* (New York: Harper & Row, 1973).

dentally, that the world Conference on the Decade for Women held in Copenhagen in 1980 will not be too heavily oriented toward Western ideas of equal rights and opportunities for women.

6. Practical know-how and experience gained in community organization in various parts of the world, including the use of mass media, could be of great value in this context.

The ideas I have presented concerning local development and the active participation of people themselves have already found acceptance in various parts of the world. I cite a few brief examples.

The Sarvodaya Shramadana movement in Sri Lanka has shown how village communities can improve their own living standards by means of small-scale development projects and appropriate technology. Local religion and philosophy also play an important role. The villagers work together in Shramadana work camps, thus promoting the process of awareness and the individual involvement of the local community (Sarvodaya).

The Harambee movement in Kenya is another excellent example of the more informal type of community development, in which emphasis is placed on self-help programs.

Examples of decentralization and local self-government are to be found in Asia, Africa, and Latin America. In China, development planning and implementation powers are delegated to the provincial county communes and brigades. More than twenty million local cadres function as a communications network between the national leaders and the local communities. Moreover, officials and technicians working in higher levels of government in China are sent out to live, work, and learn among the farming people in the villages.

The participation of the community is one of the basic principles underlying the Ujaama village development program in Tanzania. The village council and village assembly make decisions on matters concerning the community, agricultural production, education, culture, welfare, and infrastructural requirements.

Another means of promoting local participation in developing countries is the use of paraprofessionals, people with a certain amount of basic education who have proved their worth in a large number of specialized areas: for example, the "barefoot doctors" of China and the model farmers in the Comilla project in Bangladesh.

The participation of the citizen in the development of local communities is constitutionally guaranteed in Yugoslavia, which serves perhaps as a unique example of how in Europe governmental machinery, especially at the local level, provides a complex of opportunities for the direct involvement of the people in local development. These opportunities include voters' meetings, local committees, referendums, workers' self-management.[12]

Finally, I am not speaking as a social scientist or as a social philosopher, but as a social policy adviser. Thus I have a few practical suggestions for local development:

1. Local development should be given more material and moral support, both within individual countries themselves and in the agencies for bilateral and multilateral aid.

2. Local development will have to be approached more systematically within the framework of that aid.

3. The approach to rural development is still too one-sided. Two thousand million people live in rural areas, 800 million of whom are classified as destitute.[13]

4. Aid—both technical and financial—should be spread over several years and be concentrated on one region at a time.

5. The knowledge and experience available in the regions and subregions should be mutually exchanged between countries. This is more effective than making available the services of experts with a totally different cultural and social background.

6. National governments should have more faith in, and make greater use of, voluntary organizations operating in dif-

[12] Gradus Hendriks, "Role of Local Authorities in Encouraging and Supporting Citizens' Participation in the Development of Local Communities," a working paper prepared for the Economic and Social Council Asia and Pacific Regional Workshop on Methods and Techniques of Promoting People's Participation in Local Development, December, 1977.
[13] World Conference on Agrarian Reform and Rural Development, Rome, 1979.

ferent areas. Cooperatives, professional associations, women's organizations, and the like often win the confidence of the population more readily than do governmental organizations.

7. Such voluntary social welfare organizations deserve the financial and moral support of national governments.

8. These voluntary organizations, which operate at the international level, such as the ICSW, should also be provided with the necessary UN support. This is another point urged by the *ad hoc* group to which I referred earlier.

9. Nongovernmental organizations, which are often better informed about international developments and agreements, can also play an important role in advising the political and administrative authorities in their own countries.

To sum up, I would say that the concept of an international development strategy could be reformulated to cover a local, people-oriented development strategy. If the developments we have noted continue to follow the same course, social welfare will take on a new dimension which could imply a shift toward greater awareness of the individual in society.

We may be called the "soft sector" of society, and perhaps we are: we have no elitist or power structures behind us. People are our motivating force, and that is sufficient. So let us go back to people and hence to ourselves.

Summary and Review of the XXth International Conference on Social Welfare

JAMES R. DUMPSON
ASSISTANT DIRECTOR, NEW YORK COMMUNITY TRUST, UNITED STATES

RECOGNITION MUST be taken at the outset of the impossibility of submitting a summary that reliably reports the range of issues, policies, and programs that the theme of this conference suggests. Each of us brought to the conference a body of experience as well as expectations of insights and information to be gained by the exchanges we have shared. Each one of us will take back to our country what seems most relevant and useful to our individual situation. This presentation will identify the issues that emerged in the plenary sessions and in the table discussions. Further, I shall report in the context of the conference theme the general recommendations for redefinition or refinement of social policy and service delivery restructuring in the several service delivery systems; the new definition of the role of community and participation as efforts are made to improve the life experience of the disadvantaged in each of our countries. Finally, I shall also report the recommendations for program activities and social action on the part of ICSW through its national and regional structures. I believe that no one can responsibly communicate to others the depth of commitment to improving human well-being that was reflected in the attendance at the plenary sessions, or the fervor and excitement that one sensed on entering the rooms in which the table discussions were held. And only each of you can know the support, the warmth of relationship that was experienced in the many informal discussions that were held outside any formally structured meeting.

The report is presented in four parts:

Summary and Review of the Conference 183

1. A brief restatement of the most significant findings of the overview of the world social situation as reported by the five regional rapporteurs and synthesized in the working document for the conference
2. A recall of the perspectives and insights that were presented in the three plenary sessions and in the statement presented at the René Sand Award ceremony
3. A summary of the issues findings and general recommendations of the table discussions
4. A set of recommendations made as action strategies specifically for the ICSW and its national committees.

As conference rapporteur, I was most ably assisted throughout the preparation of this report by a working party of experts in the field of social development to whom I am deeply grateful. They assisted in analyzing and organizing the detailed reports of the conference section rapporteurs, in summarizing the rich perspectives and insights of the plenary sessions, and in reviewing the conclusions and recommendations. The members of the working party of experts were:

William A. Dyson, Executive Director, Vanier Institute of the Family, Ottawa, Canada; speaker of Plenary Session III

Adrian C. M. De Kok, Director, Research and Policy Planning, Social Development of the Netherlands Ministry of Cultural Affairs, Recreation, and Social Welfare; regional rapporteur for Europe, Middle East, and Mediterranean Area

John F. Jones, chairman, Board of Studies in Social Work, Chinese University of Hong Kong

David Scott, Deputy President, Australian Council of Social Services; Rapporteur for the ICSW Conference in Jerusalem

Lawrance H. Thompson, Secretary, Japanese National Committee of the ICSW; regional rapporteur for Asia and Western Pacific.

When the five regions of the ICSW reported on conditions concerning "Social Development in Times of Economic Uncertainty," on rural and urban aspects of the issues, on the needs of vulnerable groups, and the least advantages as well as the emerging phenomenon of consumerism, several significant statements became apparent:

1. While economic and social development are mutually dependent, both industrialized and less developed countries are in the midst of economic stagnation. A careful choice and conscious tradeoff among social welfare programs will need to be made. The question will arise and must be answered: What is desirable and what is affordable?

2. In all countries, those technologically developed and those less developed, a primary issue arises as to the availability and distribution of resources: Who gets what and how?

3. Social development in the context of individual, or organizational, and societal change must be viewed in relation to industrially developed and developing nations.

4. However social development is defined, whether in micro or macro terms, its goal and substance are the welfare of people, as determined by the people themselves, and the consequent creation or alteration of institutions so as to create and improve the capacity of people to meet human need and to improve the quality of human relationships between people and their societal institutions.

5. Welfare and happiness cannot be measured by levels of income. Levels of social justice and equity are essential components in determining human well-being.

6. In a period of economic uncertainty such as is likely to characterize over half of the 1980s the challenge of improving the inherent capacity of people to realize their full potential and to alter societal institutions that block achievement of this goal may be all but overwhelming. That it be achieved, however, is crucial for those who are already at risk, who live near or at the poverty level in towns and villages in all areas of the world.

7. This closing statement of the "Overview" in the Conference Working Document bears further consideration as we move ahead in considering the special findings and recommendations in the areas of housing; work, employment, and job creation for vulnerable groups; education and health for

all people; health care; personal social services; income support; services for special groups; and finally the structure and organization of the social welfare systems and the policies that are developed to insure social and economic development. There is likely to be a long-time period of economic uncertainty and for large numbers of the world's population the prospect is bleak.

THE PLENARY SESSIONS

It is of great interest that all three plenary session speakers, as well as the recipient of the René Sand Award, did not see the current world economic difficulties as the critical variable in furthering social development. All were equally aware that the planetary problems of dire poverty and widespread underdevelopment are as yet unresolved. All made it clear that despite economic advances over recent decades which continued to improve economic living levels in the industrialized nations and which assisted some countries to cross the line or approach it, the basic economic inequalities remain. Moreover, in recent times, growth has slowed considerably. Even in the "good times" solutions remain distant for half the planetary population.

Since the presentations of the plenary sessions speakers are available in this volume, only passing mention will be made here.

John F. Jones of Hong Kong, saw the need for an international master plan. He favored the work and recommendations of the Brandt Commission, but was skeptical of its implementation due to its dependence on international accord, which is now lacking. Rather he preferred to count upon the actual workaday plans of government striving to cope with the issues of development. Inasmuch as the issues facing the people of China are more representative of the underdeveloped people of the planet, he favored the orientation approaches of the People's Republic as instructive, if not as a model for others.

Senator Andre Franco Montoro of Brazil similarly illustrated the extreme poverty suffered not only by people living in nonindustrialized societies, but also in nations at a "middle level" of industrial development such as Brazil, Mexico, Peru, the Philippines, and Turkey. In such countries, the upper 10 percent of the people enjoy four to five times the national per capita income, while the lowest 40 percent enjoy just 0.25 percent of the same per capita.

William A. Dyson of Canada also began by pointing out today's excessive economic and social discrepancies. However, he placed the industrial culture of Western industrialized nations totally in question. He did not see either economic or political adjustment as the road to another and better development, so long as the belief and attitude structures remained unchanged. Rather, his view expanded on a theme also noted in the European report.

Gradus Hendriks of the Netherlands, winner of the René Sand Award, held a similar view. Accepting the need for a new international economic order, he placed the primary road to development squarely on a need for "getting back to people."

THE TABLE DISCUSSIONS

An attempt has been made to capture the most relevant content of the table discussions as reported by the rapporteurs of the three sections, which embraced all ten of the topics previously referred to, and the summaries prepared for French-, Spanish-, and Japanese-speaking participants.

TOPIC A: THE PROVISION OF HOUSING WITHIN A LIVABLE ENVIRONMENT

Housing is to be regarded as a basic human right even though few countries have been able to provide adequate housing to most of their people. Adequate standards for housing involve complex interdisciplinary considerations beyond basic space requirements now outlined by the International Labor Organization. The range of considerations would include land resources, energy resources, community development, financial resources, population changes, availability of building materials, and ideological restrictions, as well as careful coordination with each of the eight service areas serving as an outline for this report.

The universality and multifaceted nature of the housing problem implies a major role for government as the agency with overall responsibility for the well-being of a nation's people. At the same time, government involvement also implies restrictive selectivity. It is the role of the private sector, and thus of the ICSW, to assure that the restrictive selectivity of government always comes under critical scrutiny by the general public and the implementation of housing policy always involves the imaginative participation of a broader and varied perspective, close to the needs of individuals and communities within society.

The unique need of rural areas of the world are often neglected. In view of the vast populations living in these areas, frequently at the lowest levels of economic advantage, particular consideration needs to be given to the special characteristics of housing needs in rural areas, some general strategies to the end of a creative and balanced public/voluntary policy approach would include:

1. Clear articulation of the division of responsibility between public and private sectors
2. Commitment to a housing policy consciously related to other service systems (employment, education, health, income security, personal social services, and so forth)
3. Commitment to providing a range of options within any comprehensive housing policy
4. Provision of consumer participation in developing, monitoring, and revising housing policy.

TOPIC B: WORK AND EMPLOYMENT OPPORTUNITIES FOR VULNERABLE GROUPS

At each successive ICSW conference reports indicate a worsening of the employment situation in all regions. This trend is accentuated as more countries are faced with times of economic restraint. In the economically developed world, low economic growth, inflation, and advanced technology are eroding employment. Technology creates new jobs but destroys more than it creates.

Those who suffer most from unemployment are the young, women, the handicapped, and ethnic and racial minorities who are at the end of lengthening job lines. There is a need to control the application of technology to minimize its job-reducing effects, and to insure that the economic benefits are shared by providing more adequate income replacement for those who are no longer able to obtain conventional employment. Expansion of the public sector, which also helps to stimulate the private sector, would create more jobs, particularly in human services where there are often shortages of workers.

Manpower planning to predict the nature and extent of future job requirements and to determine appropriate training and retraining programs must be given higher priority.

In some countries there is evidence of greater job selectivity as a result of increased job expectations. However, the desire to be a useful participating member of society is still a universal human characteristic. Jobs that are dangerous or unpleasant should be automated where possible, or conditions improved, or their wages increased to compensate for danger or unpleasantness.

In economically developing countries, unemployment is caused by the introduction of more capital-intensive methods of production, low economic growth, and population increase. In rural areas, small-scale farming is becoming uneconomical because of the reducing size of landholdings and the increased cost of modern farming techniques. This forces families to abandon their farms and join the unemployed and underemployed in the cities.

Assistance should be given to small farmers to help them increase productivity. Any technology that is introduced to produce goods or provide services should be appropriate to levels of skill available and to employment needs.

Transnational corporations, obedient to their own economic imperatives, are an international reality. They create some jobs and destroy others. Their policies should be subject to national control if their activities are detrimental to the interests of a host country, particularly as they affect employment.

In all countries, people at local levels must be encouraged to identify ways in which more useful jobs can be created.

National committees of the ICSW should identify the causes and consequences of unemployment, develop new policies that emphasize popular involvement, and work actively to have them adopted.

TOPIC C: EDUCATION FOR ALL PEOPLE

Education is essential to self-realization, to gain access to most employment, and to enable people to communicate with others. It also helps people to understand the changes needed in values and policies in times of rapid social and economic transition.

The right to education is accepted universally, but access is still denied, or is limited, in many countries. Women, the handicapped, and minority groups such as aboriginal and tribal people have most difficulty in enjoying educational opportunities.

In economically developing countries where public resources are limited, the lack of staff and facilities reduces access to education. Experiments in providing low-cost education and training, including the use of voluntary and part-time teachers, should be encouraged.

In some countries educational content still reflects Western influences. In all countries it should be appropriate to the local culture, encouraging human values and critical faculties. It should not be designed for privileged minorities.

In times of economic restraint, there is pressure to reduce public expenditure on education and to eliminate or restrict components that do not have an occupational purpose.

It is necessary to insure that education equips people to obtain jobs that are available, but its purpose in providing people with the ability to live happily and usefully in a complex society must be recognized and maintained.

In all countries centralization or decentralization is a key issue. There seems to be general agreement that common standards are necessary, but that flexibility should be insured to meet changing needs.

Schools that experiment with new educational approaches and provide a range of choice for parents and children have an important role in a comprehensive education program.

Educational policy should not be left to educational professionals. People with other skills and interests should be involved in developing educational policies.

It is recommended that social workers, who have been traditionally concerned with the well-being of handicapped people and minority groups, should be actively involved in advocating ready access and improved quality of education for these groups.

National committees of the ICSW can help to improve the content of education and access to educational opportunities by alerting their societies to educational needs, and promoting consultation that involves all sectors of the community.

TOPICS D AND E: HEALTH FOR ALL PEOPLE; PERSONAL HEALTH CARE AND HEALTH CARE FOR SPECIAL GROUPS

The World Health Organization's goal of health for all people by the year 2000 is seen as an appropriate objective to which commitment needs to be reconfirmed. The self-perpetuating high status of the medical professions with resulting high cost, inaccessibility, and maldistribution of service is seen as the major issues to be dealt with.

A second important issue is the isolation of health care services from the concept of the whole person. An aspect of this problem is the tendency to deal with health from a pathological rather than a preventive or health developmental perspective.

A third health issue is the growing concern with the relation of illness, accidents, and physical deterioration to life style (smoking, alcohol, drugs, overeating, lack of exercise) or to nutrition and hygiene habits influenced by limited opportunity (use of powdered milk in developing countries, fast foods, and so on).

A concerted effort by all levels of related personnel will be required to deal with these issues. General recommendations are:
1. Reassessment of training to produce medical and health personnel with more generalized and/or preventive skills
2. Decentralization of planning for services and the restructuring of health-provision methods in a way that will respond to the needs of people at the local level
3. Setting priorities and reallocating funds from defense spending and high-technology investment funds to promote more effective distribution of resources
4. Provision of a challenge to doctors, paramedics, and social workers to demythologize their activities in order to eliminate unnecessary professionalism and attack the profit motive
5. Recognition of the validity of implementing "positive discrimination" in allocation of resources to special geographical areas, particular health programs, or particular consumer groups, where these measures are needed to achieve essential results.

Proposals to the ICSW include:

1. The ICSW should continue its international deliberative function, upgrade its research capabilities, and promote an increased information and skill exchange capacity.

2. "Advocacy" and "network" roles require that the ICSW work actively with related specialized agencies (the International Association of Schools of Social Work [IASSW], the International Federation of Social Workers [IFSW], etc.) to promote operational minimal cost levels of primary health care, using the services of designated liaison personnel.

3. "Advocacy," "network," and "consultative" roles with government and intergovernmental agencies should be used to influence the establishment of basic health standards, involvement in activity in the International Youth Development Project, and to influence national family policy, again using the services of designated liaison personnel.

TOPIC F: PERSONAL SOCIAL SERVICES

Personal social services are defined universally as those social provisions designed to give access preferably directly to individuals, families, and groups in their communities for preventive, rehabilitative, and developmental functions.

In all countries, but especially in developing nations, there is need for the integration of personal social services to make maximum use of scarce resources. Duplication of services appears wasteful even when it may really be a measure to deliver services to special groups, such as ethnic minorities or the handicapped. Overlap should be avoided, or, when duplication is essential, its necessity should be demonstrated. Integration applies to both the public and the voluntary sector.

The planning of personal social services calls for the social worker to be a catalyst who should insure the participation of the service recipient and allow the recipient's own voice to be heard. In the delivery of services, the indigenous culture should be respected where it is not bound to an oppressive social structure or made the excuse for an elitist system of service distribution.

TOPIC G: INCOME-SECURITY MEASURES

Income-security measures cover a host of methods meant to insure the distribution, redistribution; and *generation* of income by various means. It does not automatically follow that, because of economic problems, income-security programs should be cut. Poverty does not have a positive impact on any economy and can too easily become a vicious circle. Retrenchment is illusionary where it fosters a no-growth situation and is cruel where it calls for the poor to curb their consumer tendencies, demanding instead a deescalation of existing benefits. (In facing issues of consumerism, let the affluent, industrialized nations be especially wary of demanding sacrifice of the Third World in the name of frugality.) Income security must provide for basic needs: food, clothing, housing, education, and health. Rural communities require these no less than urban ones, although this is often forgotten in national planning.

TOPIC H: INTEGRATIVE COMMUNITY SERVICES FOR SPECIAL SECTORS

The very location of this conference brings to mind the plight of displaced people—a euphemism for refugees. The ICSW believes that refugees are an international problem and insists that it is the responsibility of all nations, especially the affluent ones, to provide for their resettlement. The conference participants pointed out that among the refugees are groups with special problems over and above the common, terrible difficulties of not being welcome anywhere. These groups include the old, the rich, the physically and emotionally handicapped. In planning integrated services for refugees it is imperative that voluntary agencies participate, especially at the local level. One method of doing this is to encourage community people as well as earlier refugees to aid in the adjustment process of resettlement.

TOPICS I AND J: THE SOCIAL WELFARE SYSTEM; POLICY ISSUES FOR SOCIAL AND ECONOMIC DEVELOPMENT

This section dealt more horizontally and globally in the macrosense with the structure and organization of the social welfare system and with Topic J, "Policy Issues for Social and Economic Development." A more or less general conclusion was that the least advantaged groups, including ethnic minorities, affected negatively by systems which fail to provide for their basic needs (as above formulated), deserve deep concern and attention in the development policy-making of international and national bodies.

Emphasis is laid further, as much as possible, on people's participation stimulated by grass-roots education and involvement in the development process.

The role of the social workers should also be considered in this context. Certain points were stressed:

There should be avoidance of overprofessionalization which

makes people more dependent on the welfare bureaucracies, as is the case in many advanced welfare states. Therefore, self-help, voluntary action, and use of paraprofessionals have to be encouraged.

For all these priorities the ICSW should act "as the world's conscience," especially in this time of economic constraints. The ICSW should let their so-called "independent voice" be heard more and more, in this way strongly influencing mentalities, attitudes of individuals and groups, policies and politics on worldwide, international, and national levels.

The continuing debate over social development policies really means that the well-being of the people, especially the least advantaged, has to be intensively stimulated by the ICSW.

Two recommendations concern directly the United Nations. First, the ICSW should request that the UN develop a resource center for information, technical assistance, and research in favor of the developing countries.

Second, the ICSW should request the UN to develop a corps to investigate and report on the plight of nations (or of people within nations), to see that their basic needs are met.

In addition, there are two special recommendations to the ICSW. First, there is a need for manpower training in the developing countries themselves, to avoid further brain drain. Second, the negative social values of consumer products have to be counteracted through education and organizing lobbies and campaigns.

RECOMMENDATIONS

Six recommendations were ICSW-specific. They were submitted by several groups who expressed a keen interest in the development of program and action strategies by the ICSW through its national committees. In submitting these recommendations no reference was made to the structural arrangements required in terms of the relation of the responsibility of ICSW headquarters in Vienna for the central coordination required in a unitary concept of the ICSW as was implied when each of these recommendations was submitted. Further, no reference was made to resource development and allocation and program evaluation, so essential for assuring the implementation and effectiveness of the recommendations. With these considerations in mind, I set forth the recommendations as they were submitted:

1. The ICSW should serve as a clearinghouse for information and social services for its national committees and through them to its total world membership.

2. The ICSW should seek to influence the development of social policy in countries in which the ICSW is represented by its national committees. In this effort, the ICSW should seek to have social welfare become one of the top priorities in each of the countries.

3. It is recommended that there be a systematic distribution of ICSW reports to international and intergovernmental bodies as well as a reverse provision of intergovernmental reports to ICSW organizations.

4. The ICSW should provide leadership in the development of a series of specialized standards for the care, support, and/or protection of the most vulnerable groups in our society—the elderly, the disabled, displaced persons, women and children, ethnic minorities, and those living in special economic or geographic circumstances.

5. The ICSW should develop both educational materials suitable for training policy-makers and materials to guide consumers in the use of a variety of community facilities as well as for participation in community planning.

6. The ICSW should facilitate the exchange of manpower and assist in providing a network of personnel equipped with the knowledge and skills for working at a variety of levels in social development, particularly in industrially developing and underdeveloped countries. A closer working relationship with the IASSW and the IASW is clearly indicated.

Obviously, these recommendations, not unlike those that conclude the reports of the table discussions, require clarification as to intent and means. The constraints of time denied this rapporteur the opportunity to pursue either the intent or the proposed means for implementation of the recommendations. They are included in this summary report for whatever action is deemed appropriate by the several organs of the ICSW.

As I come to the close of this attempt to present the spirit, concern, and commitment to the human well-being of people around the world, particularly those who are least advantaged and are likely to remain so as the world's economy continues to stagnate, I return to a priority subject for all of us in this conference. I refer to our concern and commitment to the most vulnerable of people in the world's population—the 16-odd million refugees and displaced persons in the world. They are most truly the world's have-nots; they are the most povertystricken populations living chiefly in economically and industrially developing nations. They are children, the elderly, families whose plight is due to no cause of their own. They reflect, as I quoted in the basic working document, "the unequal distribution of wealth and populations in the world," overlaid to be sure with political, technical, ideological, and legal issues. But they are human beings entitled to the same human well-being provisions that have been discussed in all the sessions of the conference. For me, a major recommendation must go abroad from the conference that overpopulation, hunger, and homelessness require international arrangements starting with measures designed ultimately to redistribute the resources of this world on an international basis.

No country, particularly those with material abundance, notwithstanding times of economic uncertainty, can justifiably renounce by word or action its economic and moral responsibility for the resettlement and placement of the world's refugees. The needs of the refugees in the world—in Africa, Asia, Europe, Latin America, and the Middle East—are real and present; they represent a serious and immediate challenge, particularly to the relatively affluent nations of the North. How the needs of the 16-odd million refugees and displaced persons are met, the nature of international protection afforded them, and the quality of services provided to them *now* may be an important harbinger for those of us who have participated in the XXth ICSW Conference, it may be an indication of the willingness and ability of the nations of the world to deal humanely and effectively with the needs of those disadvantaged people about whom we have spoken, even in a period of continuing economic uncertainty. Each of us and each of our countries are called upon to meet this challenge.

Appendix

COUNTRIES REPRESENTED AT THE XXTH INTERNATIONAL CONFERENCE OF THE INTERNATIONAL COUNCIL ON SOCIAL WELFARE

Algeria
Argentina
Australia
Austria
Bangladesh
Belgium
Belize
Brazil
Brunei
Canada
Chile
Cyprus
Denmark
Ecuador
Egypt
Fiji
Finland
France
Germany
Ghana
Greece
Hong Kong
India
Indonesia
Ireland
Israel
Italy
Ivory Coast

Jamaica
Japan
Kenya
Korea
Liberia
Macao
Mauritius
Nepal
Netherlands
Nigeria
New Zealand
Norway
Peru
Philippines
Portugal
Senegal
Sierra Leone
Singapore
Somalia
South Africa
Spain
Sri Lanka
Sudan
Surinam
Sweden
Switzerland
Taiwan
Tanzania

Thailand
Uganda
United Kingdom
United States

Venezuela
Zambia
Zimbabwe

INTERNATIONAL COUNCIL ON SOCIAL WELFARE

EXECUTIVE COMMITTEE

President
  Lucien Mehl, *France*
Vice-Presidents
  Y.F. Hui, *Hong Kong*
  Dorothy Lally, *United States*
  Robert A.B. Leaper, *United Kingdom*
  Maritza Navarro, *Panama*
  M.C.A.F. Ndiaye, *Gabon*
Treasurer-General
  Jimmy Verjee, *Kenya*
Assistant Treasurers-General
  Moacyr V.C. de Oliveira, *Brazil*
  Herbert Drapalik, *Austria*
  Mary M. Omitowoju, *Nigeria*
  Yuichi Saito, *Japan*
  Edward Weaver, *United States*
Members
  Carmen T.R. d'Arago, *Venezuela*
  Kayissan C. Brenner, *Togo*
  Anne Marie Buysse, *Belgium*
  Felicidad R. Catala, *Puerto Rico*
  Zenab I. El-Naggar, *Egypt*
  Audun Ervik, *Norway*
  Rosalind O. Forde, *Sierra Leone*
  Sybil Francis, *Jamaica*
  Lalfalbo D. Gassinta, *Chad*
  Ralph I. Goldman, *International Organizations*
  Harold Ho, *Hong Kong*
  Hak-Mook Kim, *Korea*
  Moshe Kurtz, *Israel*
  R. Bwembya Lukutati, *Kenya*
  Roy Manley, *United Kingdom*
  Salvador M. Manzanos, *Mexico*
  James Murray, *Ireland*
  Chimanbhai J. Patel, *India*
  Helen Ren, *Taiwan*
  Renate Schaefer, *West Germany*
  David Scott, *Australia*
  Teresita L. Silva, *International Organizations*
  Richard B. Splane, *Canada*
  Fred G. Stafleu, *Netherlands*
  Herman D. Stein, *International Organizations*
  S.C. Tang, *Singapore*
  Simone A. Tchinah, *Ivory Coast*
International Advisory Board
  G. d'Autheville, *France*
  Reuben C. Baetz, *Canada*
  Jan F. Beekman, *Netherlands*
  George F. Davidson, *Canada*
  Michael Goutos, *Greece*
  Zena Harman, *Israel*
  George E. Haynes, *United Kingdom*
  Helena Junqueira, *Brazil*
  Kate Katzki, *United States*
  Carlos L. Mancini, *Brazil*
  Yuichi Nakamura, *Japan*
  Rudolf Pense, *West Germany*
  Eugen Pusic, *Yugoslavia*
  Charles I. Schottland, *United States*

PROGRAM COMMITTEE

Chairman: Harold Ho, *Hong Kong*

Members

- J.A. Ahouzi, *Ivory Coast*
- Felicidad R. Catala, *Puerto Rico*
- Anna Maria Cavallone, *Italy*
- Nelson Chow, *Hong Kong*
- Sugata Dasgupta, *India*
- K.E. de Graft-Johnson, *Ghana*
- Armaity Desai, *India*
- James R. Dumpson, *United States*
- Sybil Francis, *Jamaica*
- Zena Harman, *Israel*
- Peter Hodge, *Hong Kong*
- Y.F. Hui, *Hong Kong*
- John Jones, *Hong Kong*
- Kate Katzki, *United States*
- Dorothy Lally, *United States*
- Robert A.B. Leaper, *United Kingdom*
- Roy Manley, *United Kingdom*
- Martha J. Menya, *Kenya*
- Edith Motta, *Brazil*
- Yuichi Nakamura, *Japan*
- Maritza Navarro, *Panama*
- M.C.A.F. Ndiyae, *Gabon*
- Norbert Prefontaine, *Canada*
- Eugen Pusic, *Yugoslavia*
- Olav Riihinen, *Finland*
- Yuichi Saito, *Japan*
- Charles I. Schottland, *United States*
- David Scott, *Australia*
- Richard B. Splane, *Canada*
- John B. Turner, *United States*
- Ian Yates, *Australia*
- Lucien Mehl, *ex officio*, President, ICSW
- Ingrid Gelinek, *ex officio*, Secretary-General, ICSW
- Sharad D. Gokhale, *ex officio*, Assistant Secretary-General, ICSW

INTERNATIONAL STAFF

Secretary-General
- Ingrid Gelinek, *Austria*

Assistant Secretaries General
- Martha J. Menya, *Africa*
- Sharad D. Gokhale, *Asia and Western Pacific*
- Marie-Cecile Larcher, *Europe, Middle East, and Mediterranean Area*

EDITORS

Dorothy M. Swart   Kate Katzki

HONG KONG ORGANIZING COMMITTEE

Patron
The Governor of Hong Kong,
His Excellency Sir Murray MacLehose, G.B.E.,
K.C.M.G., K.C.V.O.

Vice-Patrons
    Helena Cheng, Supervisor,
        Oberlin College, Hong Kong
    The Hon. E.P. Ho, J.P.,
        Secretary for Social Services,
        Social Services Branch, Hong
        Kong Government
    Simon Lee, Chairman, Hong
        Kong Society for the Deaf
    Leung Sing Tak, J.P.,
        Chairman, New Territories
        Women and Juvenile Welfare
        Association, Ltd., Hong Kong
    A. de O. Sales, C.B.E., J.P.,
        Chairman, Urban Council,
        Hong Kong Government

Board of Advisers
    Chairman
        The Hon. Thomas Lee,
        C.B.E., J.P.
    Members
        Mrs. Peter Choy, J.P.
        The Hon. Dr. Ho Kam Fai
        Peter Hodge
        John Jones
    L.B. MacQuarrie
    K.L. Stumpf, O.B.E., J.P.
    Ko Siu Wah, O.B.E., J.P.,
        alternate

Local Organizing Committee
    Chairman:
        Y.F. Hui, Chairman
Honorary Treasurer:
    Henry Au
Subcommittee Chairmen:
    Chan Wong Shui Reception
    Joyce Chang Field Visits
    Nelson Chow Local
        Program
    Anna Chui Volunteers

Matthew Hon Exhibition
    and Design
Kwok Ka Chi Ceremony
Grace Wan Hospitality
Patsy Wong Public Relations

Representatives:
    L.B. MacQuarrie/ Foo Tak
        Nam ICSOW Organizing
        Committee

Chan Ching Kai IFSW
    Organizing Committee
Ko Siu Wah, O.B.E., J.P.,
    alternate

Secretariat:
    Winnifred Mary Ng
        Conference Secretary

NANCY Ngai Assistant
    Conference Secretary